|| Shree Ganeshaya Namah ||

MAHARANA

The Manek Chowk, City Palace, Udaipur
A large landscaped courtyard of lawns, shrubs and fountains fronting the main entrance steps and
doorway to the palace and museum

Print designed by H. Clerget; Photograph by M.L. Rousselet
Acc. No. 2011.T.0018

MAHARANA

THE STORY OF
THE RULERS OF UDAIPUR

Brian Masters

Mapin Publishing

Revised reprint 2012 by
Mapin Publishing Pvt. Ltd, Ahmedabad
in association with
Maharana Mewar Historical Publications Trust, Udaipur

Originally published in 1990

Simultaneously published in the
United States of America in 2012 by
Grantha Corporation
E: mapin@mapinpub.com

Distributed in North America by
Antique Collectors' Club
T: 1 800 252 5231 • F: 413 529 0862
E: info@antiquecc.com
www.antiquecollectorsclub.com

Distributed in United Kingdom and Europe by
Gazelle Book Servies Ltd.
T: 44 1524 68765 • F: 44 1524 63232
E: sales@gazellebooks.co.uk
www.gazellebookservices.co.uk

Distributed in Southeast Asia by
Paragon Asia Co. Ltd
T: 66 2877 7755 • F: 66 2468 9636
E: info@paragonasia.com

Distributed in the Rest of the World by
Mapin Publishing Pvt. Ltd
502 Paritosh, Near Darpana Academy,
Usmanpura Riverside, Ahmedabad 380013
T: 91 79 4022 8228 • F: 91 79 4022 8201
E: mapin@mapinpub.com
www.mapinpub.com

ISBN: 978-81-89995-70-6 (Mapin)
ISBN: 978-0-944142-28-8 (Grantha)
LCCN: 2012932227

Editor: Mallika Sarabhai
Copyediting: Suguna Ramanathan,
Neha Manke / Mapin Editorial
Design: Gopal Limbad / Mapin Design Studio

Production: Mapin Design Studio
Printed by Aegean Offset Printers, Delhi

BY THE SAME AUTHOR

Molière
Sartre
Saint-Exupéry
Camus—A Study
Wynyard Hall and the Londonderry Family
Dreams about H.M. The Queen
The Dukes
Now Barabbas Was A Rotter: The Extraordinary Life of Marie Corelli
The Mistresses of Charles II
Georgiana, Duchess of Devonshire
Great Hostesses
Killing for Company: The Case of Dennis Nilsen
The Swinging Sixties
The Passion of John Aspinall
Gary
The Life of E. F. Benson
Voltaire's Treatise on Tolerance (translated and edited)
The Shrine of Jeffrey Dahmer
Masters on Murder
The Evil That Men Do
'She Must Have Known': The Trial of Rosemary West
Thunder in the Air: Great Actors in Great Roles
Getting Personal: A Biographer's Memoir
Second Thoughts
The Actors (Vol 1 of Garrick Club History)

CONTENTS

Acknowledgements   8

Preface by Judge Maharaj Nagendra Singh   11

Maharana Fateh Singh   26

From Bappa Rawal to the First Sack of Chittor   36

Kumbha, Sanga, and Panna Dhai   48

The Foundation of Udaipur and the Glory of Pratap   58

The Period of Construction: Maharana Jagat Singh   68

Arrival of the British   76

Victorian Stability   88

Back to Fateh Singh   102

Independence   112

Into the Future   129

The Concept of Custodian   144

The City Palace   160

Genealogical List of the Rulers of Mewar   166

Sources and Bibliography   173

TO THE MEMORY OF BHAGWAT SINGH MEWAR

ACKNOWLEDGEMENTS

My first debt of gratitude is eagerly made to Lady Selina Hastings, who first suggested I might be competent to attempt a sketch of the Mewar dynasty and thus opened to me a whole area of which I had previously been entirely ignorant.

Undeterred by my novitiate status, Shriji Arvind Singh Mewar generously made available to me documents which he controls and spent many hours discussing his family history with me, as well as making arrangements for me to visit places associated with that history. Further, he and his wife, Princess Vijayraj, permitted me to work in the tranquil surroundings of their home at Shiv Niwas Palace and offered every kind of assistance with unfailing courtesy. No expression of gratitude on my part can possibly match their kindness.

I should like to record my appreciation for the use of letters in the Royal archives at Windsor Castle, England, which are reproduced by gracious permission of Her Majesty Queen Elizabeth II.

In Udaipur, I am especially indebted to Pandit Ghanshyamlal Sharma, who shared his extensive knowledge with me on many occasions and pointed me towards many books of which I had been unaware. I was also given considerable help by Mr Subramanian, Director of the Central Office, Shiv Niwas Palace; Mr Rajendra Singh Kushwaha, Manager of Shiv Niwas Palace; Mr Tulsinath Dhabai of the City Palace Museum; Dr Menaria, Director of the Maharana Mewar Research Institute; Mr Sarin, Manager of the Motor Garage; Mr Sanjay Mukerjee, Private Secretary to Arvind Singh Mewar; Mr Deepak Dutt, Manager of the Lake Palace Hotel;

Mr Justice Peri; and Major Raghubir Singh, Manager of City Palace Museum. I trust they will all accept my thanks collectively expressed. In England, I should like to thank Virginia Fass and Andrew Topsfield, who separately assisted me with much useful information, and Philippa Scott, who offered constant encouragement and listened to the developing text with exemplary patience.

Finally, the staff at Shiv Niwas Palace all willingly came to my aid at every opportunity and helped turn the task into a treasured experience and memorable pleasure.

B.M., 1988

For this second edition, I have been given further valuable assistance, in particular by two gentlemen whose combined experience of the advances made by the House of Mewar in the intervening twenty-three years is indispensable to any historian. Thakur Bhupendra Singh of Auwa and Dr Mayank Gupta are both Deputy Secretaries of the Maharana of Mewar Charitable Foundation, the first in Administration and the second in Development. Bhupendra Singh's knowledge of the City Palace is without parallel and his familiarity with the long line of rulers in Mewar almost personal, while Dr Gupta's involvement in all projects undertaken in recent years is profound. I am grateful for the guidance and enthusiasm of each of them.

Mr H A Subramanian, Vice-President-PR, HRH Group of Hotels, has given gracious response to my every enquiry, making the writing of this edition all the more pleasant an endeavour.

Sir Stephen Lamport, KCVO, DL, Receiver General at Westminster Abbey, has clarified the constitutional position of the British monarchy and helped me avoid some egregious errors, for which I am most grateful.

Shriji Arvind Singh Mewar has once again extended to me his legendary generous hospitality, in response to which mere gratitude will never suffice, and he has allowed me the precious freedom to select, from the vast amount of material available, those subjects which I judge to be most relevant to the scope, style and purpose of this book. I can only hope that I have chosen well.

B.M., 2012

PREFACE

By Judge Maharaj Nagendra Singh*

President of the International Court of Justice

I consider it a great privilege to be associated with the illustrious house of Mewar. The house has a glorious historical past, outstanding not only for its valour and chivalry, but also for the spirit of sacrifice it displayed in the cause of the country's independence.

My *locus standi* to write this preface is manifold. The kind request from the author is backed by that of Arvind Singh Mewar, a worthy son of Maharana Bhagwat Singhji. Aside from this, I belong to the Dungarpur ruling family, connected to the Sisodia clan by an interesting episode. The episode dates back to the 11th century when the then Maharana was on his death-bed. He wanted his younger son to succeed him and not the eldest, as he felt the younger would be a better successor to the *gadi* of Shree Eklingnath ji. The eldest son came to know of his father's wishes, expressed on his death-bed. This moved him to act in keeping with the tradition of sacrifice and obedience to the command of the father, the ruler and Maharana of Mewar. He took a solemn vow to abdicate and to move out of the territories of Mewar without ever again eating or drinking water in his ancestral state, to enable the dying Maharana's wishes to be carried out. The Maharana admired the sacrifice and courage of his son and gave him men and arms to create a separate principality

---

* President, International Court of Justice; M.A., LLD. (Cantab); M.A., B.Litt., LLD. (Dublin); D.C.L. (Delhi); D.L. (Beijing); D.Sc. (Law; Moscow); D.Litt. D.Phil. (Cal); Fellow, St. John's College, Cambridge; Master Bencher, Gray's inn, London; Fellow of the British Academy; Member, Constituent Assembly of India, 1947; Member of the U.N. World Commission on Environment & Development; President of the Indian Society of International Law; President of the National Labour Law Association of India; Chancellor of the University of Goa; Freedom of the City of Salta (Argentina); LL.D. Hony. (Cordoba, Argentina). Died 1989.

RAJASTHAN

...... District Boundary
-·-· International Boundary

for himself, which the eldest son established just outside the Mewar territories. This is the origin of the Ruling House of Dungarpur, known as the Maharawals of Vagad. My eldest brother was the ruler of Dungarpur from 1918 to 1948, when the State merged in the Union of Rajasthan. Another version of the origin of Dungarpur is as given by the author in Chapter 3. Whatever may be the truth as to details, the fact of the abdication of the eldest son in favour of the youngest is well known in Rajasthani history and cherished as a sacrifice in obedience to the wishes of the father.

Wherever there is a Rajput population, be it in U.P., Bihar, M.P., the Punjab, or even in Europe and the Americas, the name of Mewar is revered. The names of Bappa, Kumbha, Sanga, Pratap and the great Raj Singh are sung not only in the bardic language of Rajasthan but also dramatised in Bengali, and are a source of inspiration throughout India. It is possible to write an entire book on each of the aforesaid giants of Mewar. If Kumbha ushered in a period of renaissance by encouraging art, architecture, music and learning with a spirit of tolerance unknown in his time, it is the mighty Sanga who checked the Moghul onslaughts, in the 16th century, and sacrificed all for the independence of the motherland.

Brian Masters has very rightly highlighted all these aspects in this work and made it interesting reading. There are not many books written on the House of Mewar and certainly not in recent times. The classic work on the subject is by Col. James Tod who served the cause of the British Government admirably as the Political Agent at Udaipur to the then Governor General of India. Tod became famous through his *Annals and Antiquities of Rajasthan*, and would,

I am sure, have been happy to read this narration which brings the facts of history up-to-date and covers more recent times.

History will note the remarkable sacrifice of Maharana Bhupal Singh who offered the territorial integrity of the ancient state of Mewar as the sacrificial golden fruit to bring about the unity of India. Udaipur took a leading part in the unification process by which over 565 princely states sought unity and were integrated with the Dominion of India in 1947 to help to build the present independent nation. Maharana Bhupal Singh appreciated that the fight for the independence of Mewar, spread over centuries of Indian history, had to merge with the fight for the independence of the country, and readily came forward to integrate his state to create a Union of Rajasthan States. He was rightly elected the Maharaj Pramukh i.e. the then constitutional head of the newly federated state. My eldest brother, Maharawal Lakshman Singhji, was elected Upraj Pramukh, under the Maharana's headship.

Maharana Bhagwat Singh earned a name among the long list of Maharanas by creating trusts to encourage learning and scholarship, and to give assistance to the poor and needy of the country. These trusts which perpetuate the memory of the heroes of Mewar, as well as his valuable efforts towards the economic modernisation of Udaipur, will always remain everlasting contributions to posterity.

It is gratifying to see that Arvind Singh Mewar is sincerely carrying out and maintaining the same high tradition of Mewar, implementing the wishes of his father. He now administers the trust and has brought modern expertise to augment the tourist industry by his excellent management of the several Palace Hotels of the city, created by his father.

I have no doubt that, as is only right, he is moving in the footsteps of his father and earning the blessings of their protective deity Ekling ji through scrupulous adherence to the motto of Mewar.**

** "Those who stand steadfast in upholding the law will succeed in perpetuating the glorious traditions of the family."

Parmeshwaraji Maharaj Shree Eklingnath ji, the Ruler of Udaipur, Mewar

Bappa Rawal receiving 'Mewar' from his Guru Maharishi Harit Rashi

Acc. No. 2011.T.0002

Inlay mosaic in the Mor Chowk, 19th century engraving

FOLLOWING PAGES Aerial view of the City Palace Complex, Udaipur

Aerial view of the City Palace Complex, Udaipur
Painting by Sardar S.G. Thakar Singh, 1930–35
Acc. No. 2011.25.0009_R

Shiv Niwas Palace, Udaipur

Sabhagaar, the Durbar Hall, Fateh Prakash Palace Convention Centre,
Fateh Prakash Palace, Udaipur

Maharana Fateh Singh (1884–1930)

Photograph by Bourne & Shepherd
Acc. No. 2008.06.0258

MAHARANA FATEH SINGH

Anyone who visits the enchanting city of Udaipur for the first time and finds himself a guest at the serene hill-top Palace of Shiv Niwas or the dream-like floating Lake Palace (properly called "Jagniwas"), will feel around him the spirit of a remarkable ancestry, renowned not only for its extreme antiquity, surpassing that of any European royal house, but, more importantly, for its gentle ideals and correspondingly firm tenacity in upholding them. Indeed, it is fitting that one should regard oneself as a guest at Shiv Niwas rather than a lodger, for it is part of the sacred purpose of the Hindu to bestow selfless hospitality upon the traveller. Equally, it is the solemn obligation of the Hindu ruler to protect and serve the people who depend on him as well as to administer and govern the affairs of the State. There are profound and subtle reasons for this view of the ruler as humble guardian of a trust, reasons that will become clear later. This is a view different in kind, not just in degree, from the European tradition of monarchy. For the moment it is enough to remember that the word "raja", normally translated as "king" in the original Sanskrit, combines two meanings—"he who rules", and "he whose duty it is to please". Nobody embodied the significance of this duality more movingly than the man who built Shiv Niwas Palace at the end of the nineteenth century, Maharana Fateh Singh, the revered 73rd sovereign of the State of Mewar.

To call Fateh Singh an extraordinary man is almost to belittle language. Only superlatives can adequately describe his qualities, yet only simplicity can properly convey his virtue. He was regarded by many as the last true monarch in India, by his people as not only head of all the Rajputs but virtual leader of the Hindus. His spiritual authority was as unassailable as that of the Pope for

Roman Catholics, his temporal influence so absolute that successive British Viceroys, whose power in theory superseded his, were constantly thwarted in their endeavours to undermine him. "Whatever punishment may be meted out to Udaipur", wrote one British memo, "we can never dethrone him from his position in the hearts of the Rajput people." Fateh's determination to resist British interference in the affairs of his people did not derive from mere stubbornness of character, still less from any love of power for its own sake, but from the inherited conviction that he must never allow the dignity of the House of Mewar to be impaired, and that such dignity was expressed by his inalienable responsibility towards his people. Hence a British recommendation would only be entertained by Maharana Fateh Singh if it suited the wishes and increased the happiness of the people he represented. Of that happiness he would be, and had perforce to be, the sole judge.

All of which sounds awesome and forbidding, and Fateh Singh's place in the history of India would be one among many if it rested solely on the exercise of feudal authority. So too would the respect due to his memory be ordinary if based only on his role as king and spiritual leader. But his personal qualities were such as to inspire love and admiration in all who met him, and the historian will seek in vain for any disparaging remark among those recorded memories which have come down to us. The transparent sincerity of the language used by those British people who knew the Maharana is proof enough that they cannot have been moved by any desire to express sycophantic approval. Here are but a few of them:

> "His Highness's strength and personality are so striking that who knows him or has ever once come into contact with him cannot but feel a deep veneration for him."
>
> *Sir Robert Holland*

> "His charm of manners and address, his hospitality and perfect courtesy are known beyond the borders of Rajputana. As a private gentleman of unblemished life and character, he is beyond reproach."
>
> *Sir Arthur Martindale*

"He had the most perfect manners in the world, gracious and inscrutable alike to all. It was interesting to watch the effect of his wonderful manners on diverse persons. It was a privilege merely to sit with him."

Sir Walter Lawrence

"He was one of the finest characters I have ever known, the soul of truth and honour, but very slow to decide because of the overwhelming fear of deciding wrongly."

G.E.C. Wakefield

"I have met royal persons in my life and sometimes been disappointed, but one person I shall never forget was Maharana Sir Fateh Singh of Mewar. I saw him first when he called on the Resident clad in plain and spotless white, with his up-curled Rajput beard (just as white) framing a face like smoothly wrinkled parchment. He moved with such dignity that the slightness of his figure seemed of no account. His gaze defied flattery and deceit, and, though he never raised his voice, every syllable could be heard in the hush which his calm presence created. I thought to myself that, if this was the result of nearly two thousand years of breeding and generations of personal rule, there was clearly something to be said for preserving such qualities for the future well-being of India."

Sir Conrad Corfield

"He is constitutionally incapable of deviating from the truth as he conceives it, and loyalty is inherent in his very life... quite simple, transparently honest, searching whole-heartedly for truth, but handicapped in coming to a decision by the terrible weight of his responsibilities and ancestry, he never, to my recollection, sought his own advantage in anything."

Sir Claude Hill

While the reader may be already convinced by this parade of laudatory reminiscence, yet the last testimony must belong to that most august and self-confident of Viceroys, Lord Curzon, who had scant regard for other mortals and was quick to discern and deflate vanity. Curzon as a rule liked to get down to business in his meetings with Rajput chiefs and discuss matters of administration and propose reforms, but on his first encounter with Maharana Fateh Singh even he was reduced to respectful passivity and fell completely under the man's indefinable charm. Lawrence, who was present, wrote that such was the atmosphere of courtesy that it would have been almost profane to touch upon such commonplace matters as policy. "Little was said, for the Maharana, like most great Indians of that time, believed in golden silence, and the most valuable of his visitors seemed disinclined to be talkative in that gracious and noble presence." Lawrence went on to describe Fateh Singh's manners as "divine", an apt choice of epithet, for indeed the strength of his ineffable calm derived from sources deep in the religious consciousness of man. It was easy to concur in the belief that the Maharana was "the Light of the Hindus".

For one who occupied so exalted a position, Fateh Singh emerged from relatively humble beginnings. His early years were spent as a fairly obscure rustic dweller, living the simplest of lives in a feudal village. He was uneducated and nearly illiterate. But his essential goodness and peasant piety were never in doubt. Brought up to respect the tenacious family traditions passed down through the recitations of bards and poets who kept alive the verbal literature of Mewar, Fateh's character was moulded by notions of austerity, denial of self, and subservience to the maintenance of Rajput pride. Such notions cherished the glory of Rajput independence and purity above all else, and were as much a part of his inheritance as the piety of his Hindu way of life.

He was thirty-five years old when he came to the *gadi* (throne) of Mewar in 1885 by virtue of the death of his cousin and predecessor, Maharana Sajjan Singh, without surviving children. In such an event, Rajput custom allows the adoption of another member of the clan to succeed as if he were the son and heir. This differs from the principle of primogeniture as it applies particularly in England, where the failure of a direct heir brings the titles and honours to the senior male representative descended from their original grantee.

Here, the Rajput noblemen confer with the Maharana to select a member of the clan, who is then adopted as son. He is still, nevertheless, a blood descendant of the founder of the family, thus ensuring the continuation of the line. (In 76 generations, adoptions have occurred only eight times, and they have always been taken from three close subsidiary branches of the family—more of this later.)

It happened that the adoption of Fateh Singh was a stroke of genius, for his immediate two predecessors had made compromises with the British authorities, which were thought by many to be to the Imperial advantage and to the detriment of Mewar's interests. Fateh Singh's singularity of vision reversed all that and instituted a long period of assertion which, given his strength of character, all but reduced British envoys to impotence. To the consternation of the British Resident, he sacked his *dewan* (Prime Minister)— Panna Lal—through whose discreet agency British meddling was channelled, and announced that he intended to rule alone. Thereafter, whenever he was called upon to make a decision, he would ponder it, sometimes for months on end, until he was sure in his own mind that he was acting according to justice and fairness. There were instances when his settlement of a claim by one of his people ran counter to his own predisposition, as long as evidence was found in his papers and records (which only he saw) to justify it. He would carry one course of action scribbled on a piece of paper hidden in his turban, and the opposite on another piece held behind his waistband, and destroy one only when support for the other was irresistible. It was a kind of justice by solitary Cartesian dialogue, and it worked so well that Fateh Singh was trusted as a sage.

When the British implored him to assist in drawing State boundaries (for Mewar was in his day still largely uncharted), he told them to follow the goats and draw their lines where they led. He further answered the request for a map by producing a *popadum* (the Indian crisp at the beginning of a meal), whose wrinkles, he said, would provide as accurate a map as any. He refused to allow a modern water-system to be introduced in Udaipur on the grounds that water-carriers would be thrown out of work as a result, and only relented when alternative employment was found for all of them. Firmly resolved to adhere to the principles of kingship which had endured in his land for fourteen centuries virtually without change, Maharana Fateh Singh was bound eventually to clash with the exasperated British, despite his popularity with his own people and the stability assured by such devotion. The partial curtailment of his powers by the British must wait for a later stage in our narrative. Suffice it to say for the moment that, alone among Rajput kings, he steadfastly refused to offer obeisance to the British monarch or to admit to a subservient status. He regarded King George V as, at best, an equal.

For the forty-five years of his reign, Maharana Fateh Singh forbade himself any private life. He slept with four of his *sardars* (noblemen) surrounding his bed, with replacements in rotation every two hours. At least fifty people would come to salute him every morning, and another two hundred, women and children, would be fed. He heard representations from his people and did his best to satisfy them. He lunched with one hundred people around him every day, all of them speaking with their hands over their mouths so that the Maharana should not breathe the same air as themselves. One British Resident said that he did not look upon him as a man but as a demi-god.

It is important to insist that Fateh Singh would never have regarded himself as any such thing, for the essence of Mewar kingship was rooted in a paradoxical humility. The Maharanas of Mewar (later called, erroneously, Maharanas of Udaipur) considered themselves to be *dewans*, servants, of the god Ekling ji (a manifestation of Shiva), and whatever power they possessed was due only to their being Ekling ji's earthly representatives, bound by duty and custom to serve his will and administer on his behalf. In processions, the emblem of Ekling ji was always carried at the head, the Maharana following in second

The Temple of Shree Eklingnath ji
Photograph by K.L. Syed & Co.
Acc. No. 2011.10.0166-00071

place. Through the long centuries of their history, successive Maharanas have made the pilgrimage to the temple of Ekling ji on every Monday of the year to seek guidance and counsel in barefooted prostration before their god; the Maharana is then an imperfect mortal anxious to serve the dignity of humanity in God's creation. It was always, and is still, a moving sight, and the visitor to Udaipur would advance his understanding of the history of the place were he to make the journey to Ekling ji, only half an hour's distance, where the present head of the family, Arvind Singh Mewar, still performs this ancient and sacred rite. He lives at Shambhu Niwas Palace, and can be seen leaving the palace at 6:15 p.m. on Mondays (Lord Shiva's day). No one doubts that the custom will continue, as it must, forever, no matter what political and social changes may occur.

Such, then, was the proud sense of piety which Maharana Fateh Singh brought to his task as ruler and which informed his daily life. He rose every morning at 5.00 a.m. and prayed for an hour. His habits were regular, simple, austere. He abhorred drinking and license of any sort. He married but twice, the second marriage taking place only after the death of his first wife (unlike many of his predecessors, allowed then by Hindu law to maintain several wives at once), and dedicated his whole life to a profound realisation of decent moral values. The exquisite crystal furniture which is on show now in Fateh Prakash Palace had been ordered by Maharana Sajjan Singh and was delivered from Belgium in the time of Maharana Fateh Singh. Typically, he declined to use it, as such ostentatious luxury did not sit well with the spartan simplicity which he embraced; the furniture remained in the crates in which it had arrived for over sixty years. He occupied the more modest rooms, in what is now Suite No. 5 at Shiv Niwas Palace. Similarly, he would not permit himself to eat or wash on a train ("fire carriage" he called it), but had the train stopped so that he could indulge such needs close to Mother Earth.

There are two reasons why it is fitting we should start our introduction to the history and significance of the oldest surviving dynasty in the world with this gracious and saintly man. First, because he built Shiv Niwas Palace (after foundations had been laid by his predecessor) as a guest house for his own visitors, a function which happily it still performs. Since his day, Shiv Niwas Palace has played host to Queen Elizabeth II of England, and most recently, their Royal Highnesses the Duke and Duchess of Kent. Second, because Fateh Singh was in his way the epitome of Rajput chivalry, though he fought no battles and secured no treaties. His life demonstrated with utmost clarity the difference between the traditions of European royalty, based upon acceptance of the right of kings as superior persons, and those of the Rajputs, based upon family ties between ruler and subject. Indeed, this is true in fact, not only in belief, for all Rajput families, however lowly in station, are ultimately descended from the same source and all carry the surname Singh ("lion"). Hence the Maharana of Udaipur was known affectionately by the people as *Bapu* ("Father"), *Bapuji* ("honoured father"), or *Ma-Baap* ("father and mother"). Also, the Maharana's position was never founded upon the possession of land or the ownership of castles, but on trusteeship, on the maintenance of what had been granted on trust to the ancestors. That is why it is impossible to find, throughout the many turbulent years of struggle in the battlefield, any instance of aggression on the part of Mewar. Their wars have been uniquely defensive, in obedience to the vows of honour, decency and hospitality made to the deity Ekling ji. To trace how and why these values have been held dear, we must return to the very beginnings of history in Rajasthan.

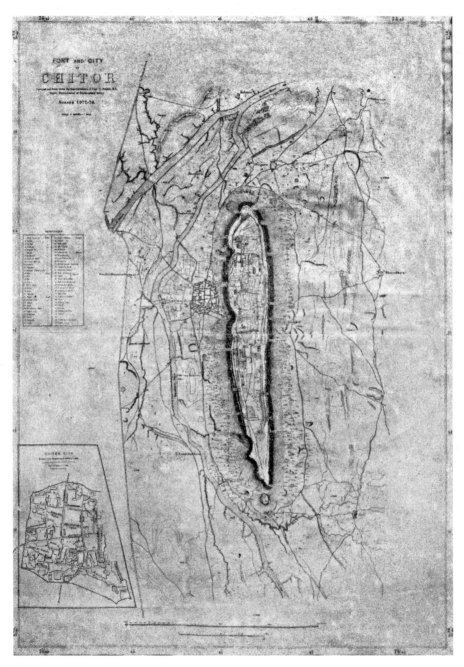

Chittor

FROM BAPPA RAWAL
TO THE FIRST SACK OF CHITTOR

Rajasthan, formerly known as Rajputana, means "the land of kings", and all Rajputs are commonly held to be the sons of kings, which implies no more than that they are ultimately descended from one of the thirty-six royal races of Rajputs established some two thousand years ago. Whence they originally came is still a matter of hot dispute among historians, but is in no way contested by bardic revelation, which states quite clearly that some families were descended from the Sun, through the god Rama ("Suryavanshis"), while others traced their beginnings to the Moon, through the god Krishna ("Chandravanshis"). The ruling family of Jaisalmer is one of the latter, and our own ruling family in Udaipur is the senior representative of the former, which is why the family crest is a blazing gold sun against a crimson background. As Colonel Tod, the first and greatest of all writers on Rajasthan, cryptically remarked, "The Rajputs are scarcely satisfied with discriminating their ancestors from the herd of mankind. Some plume themselves on a celestial origin, while others are content to be demi-celestial." A modern interpretation holds that the mythology conceals a more rational truth, namely that the first ancestor, source of all bounty, was as powerful as the Sun, source of all energy; as a consequence, he bore the name Surya—"the sun".

As for factual provenance, there are some, mostly Western, commentators who attempt to explain the emergence of the Rajputs by placing them as descendants of the hordes of Huns who came pillaging from Asia, or even as Persian invaders, but Hindi historians, on the whole, will have none of this; they aver that the forefathers were a people already established in what is now called Rajasthan. Whatever the case, it seems probable that the royal families with which we have to deal moved into the area from Kashmir in the first century A.D., and that the line latterly represented by the Mewar dynasty firmly established itself in the Aravalli hills soon afterwards.

By the time we reach the sixth century, there occurs the first of many stirring tales of survival which adorn this long epic history. In the year 525 the capital of this incipient nation was sacked by invaders and the entire ruling family wiped out, save for the chief Queen, Pushpavati, who was pregnant with the sole heir to the house. She escaped because she was on a pilgrimage when the attack took place. Pushpavati was given sanctuary by Brahmin priests in a cave of the Aravalli hills, and when the baby was born he was named Guhil (which means "cave-born"). Once sure of the succession, Queen Pushpavati had her own funeral pyre constructed and threw herself upon it to perish in the flames, having first entrusted her baby to the daughter of a temple priest, who raised and cared for him.

By the time he was eleven years old, Guhil was spending most of his days in the forest with an indigenous race called the Bhils, descendants of the original Stone Age hunters of this land, and was soon acknowledged as a natural leader and treated by them as such. One day the son of a Bhil chieftain accidentally cut his thumb, and pressing it against Guhil's forehead, marked it with his blood. This was taken to symbolise the anointing of Guhil as first of his clan, and is considered to be the origin of the *tika* mark of sovereignty on the forehead. The Bhil chieftain then granted Guhil his first territory, a stretch of forested mountain. By an astonishing longevity of custom, the Bhils retained, for the next thirteen hundred years, the right to perform this ancient grant of sovereignty, and at each investiture of a Mewar ruler it was the Bhil chieftain who drew blood from a cut on his own thumb and, after marking the ruler's forehead, led him by the arm to take his seat on the *gadi* (throne). Thus did the Mewar kings never forget that their original land was a gift, and paid tribute to this grant in each generation, considering themselves not entitled to reign until the gift was renewed. For this reason, the coronation of a new ruler always took place immediately after the death of his predecessor, without waiting for funeral rites to be observed.

Guhil founded the State of Mewar in the year 566, and his descendants, called the Guhilots, continued to rule in the same area for the next seven generations. Isolated from the rest of India by mountains and dense forests, Mewar developed the spirit of iron discipline and stoic resolve which was to become the country's most salient feature and to arm its determined resistance. Its capital was Nagda, named after the fourth ruler Nagaditya, who reigned in 626. The ruins of Nagda may still be seen some twenty miles from Udaipur, and are chiefly remarkable for a small but solidly impressive temple, one of the purest examples of sacred Hindu architecture. (It dates, alas, from some three hundred years later, c. A.D. 990.*)

The seventh ruler of the line was accidentally killed by Bhils while out hunting in 734, and the three year-old heir, known to history as Bappa Rawal, was rescued from the threat of insurrection by a Brahmin woman and protected by her in Nagda; she was even said to be a lineal descendant of the woman who had raised Guhil two hundred years before. With Bappa Rawal we come to the first great ruler of this illustrious line, and the one henceforth always to be recognised as the true founder of the family's supremacy among Rajputs. It was he who moved the capital to the mighty fortress city of Chittor.

More importantly, perhaps, he is the source of that pious humility referred to in the previous chapter as the distinguishing mark of this dynasty. The boy grew up as a simple cowherd. At some time in his youth, he met a hermit

---

* It is even possible that Nagda remained the capital until the end of the 10th century, in which case the temples still standing there would be contemporaneous with its period of greatest glory. Some historians claim there is no proof that Chittor supplanted Nagda as the capital until much later, and, relying on sparse inscriptions, have brought the date forward to the 13th century. These same historians point out that the Guhil legend of being born in a cave and rescued by a woman is repeated in many Indian genealogies relating to other families (just as the story of Jesus Christ and virgin birth occurs frequently in Middle Eastern mythology), and that no credence can be given to it. The Guhilots were more prosaically descended from a Brahman family of Anandapura (probably Ahar, near Udaipur), who married into Kshatriya families and assumed Kshatriya caste after some generations. Similarly, historians have squabbled over exactly who Bappa Rawal was, whether the 8th ruler, Kalbhoj, or the 5th ruler, Shiladitiya. There is precious little evidence to discourage these speculations.

leading the life of an ascetic in the forest, a holy sage called Maharishi Harit Rashi. He became the boy's spiritual guide. Maharishi Harit Rashi educated his charge in the principles of Hindu morality and the rites of Shiva, and taught him in particular to recognise the local deity, Ekling ji, as the supreme lord of Mewar. Eventually, he saw in the boy such religious rigour and nobility that he appointed him the vessel of Ekling ji on earth. It is from this time that all the descendants have regarded themselves as transient regents representing the people before God, and not as rulers by personal right.

When he learned that he was nephew to the deposed Prince of Chittor, the youth abandoned his shepherd's life to assume his responsibilities as head of the family. The fortress of Chittor was then held by the Mori prince of Malwa, and Bappa marched with his Bhil allies to take possession of a city which was to be the guardian of his people's independence. Apparently, there was little resistance as the Malwa noblemen were demoralised by private knowledge of Bappa's superior claim and the confidence of his supporters. The Bhils thereupon elected him as their paramount chief, vowing allegiance to him and his line in perpetuity, and indeed it was the descendants of his two Bhil cohorts who continued to apply the *tika* of sovereignty to all subsequent rulers until the nineteenth century.

That he was held not only in high esteem but also regarded with deep affection is attested by the name by which he has been known ever since—Bappa Rawal (his real name was Kalbhoj). "Bappa" means father, an intimate term of endearment, and "Rawal" is an ancient title of the Kshatriya caste, one of the four principal castes of Hinduism. Kshatriyas are warriors, whose solemn duty it is to defend the people without a thought of personal risk, the other three castes being Brahmin (priestly), Vaishya (mercantile), and Sudra (service). It was Bappa who built the first temple at Ekling ji, with an icon of granite as pure and clear as a diamond. (Hundreds of years later, it was removed and hidden in a lake to protect it from the Moghuls; it was never found again, and the present icon, in shiny black marble, is a fifteenth-century replacement.) No stone of Bappa's building remains, though there is another temple at Chittor,

Chittor, capital of Mewar for 800 years

Acc. No. 2011.T.0023

known as Kalka Mata, which probably dates from his time and may well have been erected by him.

Maharishi Harit Rashi laid down cardinal rules for Bappa to follow, based upon respect for mankind, service to the community, and maintenance of ancient Vedic culture. These precepts have never been forgotten, and are the most solid legacy which he passed on. How much of Bappa Rawal's personal story is owed to tradition and how much to accurate historical fact is difficult to disentangle, there being a paucity of reliable records with which to test it. It is said, for example, that Bappa was fifteen years old when he took Chittor, and that he lived one hundred years. This cannot be reconciled with the dates of his reign, from 734 to 753.

It is also said that his double-edged sword could sever rocks (and certainly his descendants habitually used a sword fashioned in this manner, with two edges).

Of three facts we may however be certain; that all subsequent rulers of the State of Mewar are descendants of the body of Bappa Rawal; that subservience to the deity Ekling ji dates from his time; and that the seat of administration he established at Chittor remained the capital of Mewar for the next eight hundred years.

The defence of Chittor turned out to be an onerous liability, though one which was scarcely shirked despite literally countless attempts at invasion. Throughout many of those eight hundred years Chittor was almost constantly the object of siege by ruthless Muslim conquerors attempting to convert the world to Islam by the sword, with that fierce messianic fervour which one sees even today in the Middle East. The tolerant and gentle Hindus were incredulous in the face of such absolutism, yet nonetheless determined to uphold their own faith and resist the relentless spoliation of their temples. It is quite impossible to enumerate all the battles that were fought over the next five centuries, and in any case it would be tiresome, but something of the extraordinary persistence of Bappa Rawal's progeny can be gleaned from the sonorous and impressive prose of Colonel Tod, the first Westerner to study Rajput lore in depth.

> What nation on earth [he wrote] would have maintained the semblance of civilisation, the spirit or the customs of their forefathers, during so many centuries of overwhelming depression, but one of such singular character as the Rajput? Rajasthan exhibits the sole example in the history of mankind, of a people withstanding every outrage barbarity can inflict or human nature sustain, from a foe whose religion commands annihilation, and bent to the earth, yet rising buoyant from the pressure, and making calamity a whetstone to courage... Mewar alone, the sacred bulwark of religion, never compromised her honour for her safety, and still survives her ancient limits; and since the brave Samar Singh [of the 41st generation] gave up his life, the blood of her princes has flowed in copious streams for the maintenance of this honour, religion, and independence.

Little wonder, then, that during these dark and gruesome years, Chittor became the symbol of Hindu resistance, and that its rulers acquired their reputation as ultimate guardians of Hinduism. From these times, ever alive in the folk memory of Rajasthan, dates the ascendancy of Mewar rulers as the premier race of Rajputs.

Their "finest hour" came in three separate and devastating destructions of Chittor, when their valour was put to a test too severe to imagine, and their response rose to extremes of sacrifice unmatched in any other chronicle. To the first of these, in 1303, we must now turn.

By this time, the Sultans of Delhi had been consolidating their power in India for nearly one hundred years, since the proclamation of the first Sultan in 1206. They were to last until the Moghuls took over in 1526, but the fiercest and most ambitious of them all was Ala-ud-din Khilji, who, having conquered practically the whole of northern India, had set his heart on subduing the one recalcitrant jewel, the mighty fortress of Chittor. By 1303 he was ready. The newly-anointed master of Chittor was Ratan Singh, of the 42nd generation.

In the breathless words of Charles Allen, "the history of Rajasthan is something marvellous, but the history of Chittor is above everything." The fort sits high on a flat-topped hill surrounded by thirteen kilometres of battlements so wide that a team of eight horses could gallop along their summit, abreast. Within, there were temples, colleges, palaces, bazaars, home for an entire community, plus lakes and mountain springs. Beyond and below the imposing walls, flat fertile plains. Much of this may still be seen today, on a two-hour trip from Udaipur.

Ala-ud-din laid siege to Chittor for many months in 1303, and the inhabitants were beginning to suffer from the deprivation of supplies and to wonder if their ordeal would ever cease, when Ratan Singh received from the Muslim a most astonishing message. Ratan Singh's queen was a lady of pure unsullied beauty

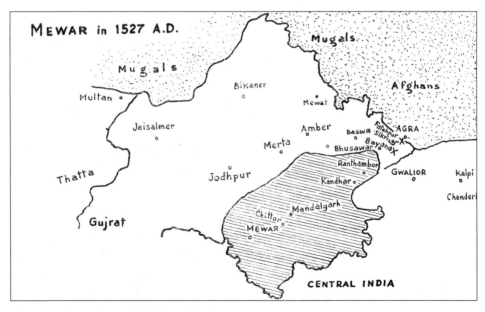

The ancient boundaries of the State of Mewar

called Padmini. Originally from Ceylon, the fame of her unparalleled beauty had preceded her and endured despite her strict observance of *purdah*, according to which every Rajput woman disappeared from view immediately after the wedding and was never seen again by any man save her husband. Ala-ud-din had heard of Padmini's legendary looks. His curiosity was aroused. Curiosity begot desperation, and desperation was mother to cunning. His message to Ratan Singh was that he would lift the siege on Chittor in exchange for one simple request—that Padmini should be surrendered to him.

Naturally, this appalling suggestion was rejected with the utmost indignation, as Ala-ud-din doubtless expected it would be. It was part of his plan that a lesser demand would appear more attractive if it replaced an impossible one. He would agree to a compromise—that he might be allowed to glimpse Padmini's image reflected in a mirror, thus preserving her honour and respecting her *purdah*. Then he would withdraw his forces.

Suspecting that this proposal might well hide a tactic designed to gain access to the fortress and thereby study its inner defences, Ratan Singh was at first hesitant, but in accordance with Rajput code of honour, he decided that the solemn word of an adversary was worthy of trust, and gave orders that Ala-ud-din be escorted through the great gates to a palace on the banks of the lake, where he could sit in a room overlooking Padmini's water-pavilion with his back to the window and a mirror on the wall opposite. This duly took place. Padmini emerged from the pavilion and descended the steps to the water's edge. Ala-ud-din spied her reflection, as was intended, and was transfixed with wonder.

Having fulfilled his part of the bargain, Ratan Singh escorted his guest back through the gates, whereupon he was seized as a prisoner, and the terms of his release dictated. Padmini must be handed over to the envious Sultan without conditions. Of course, it was inconceivable either that a Hindu queen should be joined to a Muslim harem, or that the Rajput chief should be abandoned as a prisoner. Only one solution to the dilemma could be countenanced.

Padmini announced her accession to the ultimatum, stipulating that, as befitted her rank, she should be accompanied by her ladies and household. Thus the royal palanquin made its journey to the Sultan's camp, followed by seven hundred palanquins, each screened with *purdah* curtains and carried by six bearers. Once inside the camp, Ratan Singh and his wife were permitted half an hour together to bid farewell. Thereupon, the curtains of the palanquins were drawn to reveal, not a retinue of women, but the full army of Rajput noblemen. A desperate hand-to-hand battle ensued, with hundreds of casualties on each side, but at least Ratan Singh and Padmini were enabled to reach the security of Chittor to ponder the next move. Ala-ud-din also retreated, pending reassembly of his forces for a repeat attack, humiliation corroding his soul.

Padmini and all the womenfolk, some thirteen thousand of them, bade farewell to husbands, sons and husbands-elect, donned their wedding robes and jewellery and, singing exultantly, walked into the underground tunnels and closed the doors behind them. They then built a vast funeral pyre, cast their infants into it, and finally threw themselves upon the flames. This done, the menfolk marched through the gates of Chittor to their final rendezvous, the ashes of their wives and sisters smeared on their foreheads, and wearing their saffron robes. Tod's vivid depiction of the scene conveys the awful solemnity of the occasion:

> [Ratan Singh], satisfied that his line was not extinct, now prepared to follow his brave brethren; and calling around him his devoted clans, for whom life had no longer any charms, they threw open the portals and descended to the plains, and with a reckless despair carried death, or met it, in the crowded ranks of Allah. The Tartar conqueror took possession of an inanimate capital.

It is difficult adequately to appreciate the sweet but terrible victory accomplished by this act. The ritual of *johar* (self-immolation) had preserved the women from dishonour, pollution or captivity, and robbed the conqueror of any female prize. The sacrifice of all the men further deprived him of any audience to the conquest. A conqueror must lord it over his victims, or his efforts go unnoticed. He must realise the precious pleasure of being able to gloat. Ala-ud-din had not a soul to gloat over, the smoke still rising from the funeral pyre cruelly reminding him of his failure. The Rajputs had successfully destroyed his vanity. In his frustration, he demolished everything in his path, temples, palaces, houses, sparing only Padmini's water-pavilion; (this fell to ruin much later, and the visitor may now see a replica of the original, constructed some four hundred years after the event).

Largely as a result of this ecstatic display of heroism, the leaders of Mewar re-affirmed their supremacy over all other Rajput races, a position acknowledged in the style of address which they thenceforth adopted by general approbation. While all Rajput kings were called Raja, the Mewar chief would now be known as Rana; the prefix "Maha", meaning "great", was added in the course of the next generation. There are Maharajas aplenty in Rajasthan, but there is only one Maharana. The first of the family to use this designation was the 43rd ruler, Maharana Hamir Singh (1326–1364).

The fortress of Kumbhalgarh

KUMBHA, SANGA, AND PANNA DHAI

From Hamir Singh's time dates the use of the clan name Sisodia to denote the common root of the various branches which spread the family's growing influence. "Sisodia" came from a village called Sisoda, close to the family's original seat of power. Some one hundred and fifty years before Hamir Singh, the 35th ruler, Samant Singh, had left Chittor following a military defeat and been succeeded by his younger brother Kumar Singh. Samant Singh had meanwhile founded another line of the family, bifurcating the descent, and his genes are now carried by the Maharawal of Dungarpur (technically, therefore, the senior branch of Sisodias in terms of precedence by age). No less than five royal families in Rajasthan are of the Sisodia clan, but only the head of the central branch, of Udaipur, is Maharana.

When Hamir Singh regained Chittor from the Sultan in 1326, he was the only unhampered Hindu king left in northern India. A valiant warrior and stable administrator, he inaugurated a period of relative peace and rebuilding, and for two hundred years afterwards, Chittor enjoyed the recovery and prosperity which his mild paternal government made possible. His grandson, Maharana Lakha Singh (1382–1421), continued the process, erecting wonderful temples and palaces at enormous cost. One is bound to wonder if the people ever resented this lavish expense, fed by their labour, but there is no real evidence that they did. On the contrary, they were proud of their monuments and pleased when the Maharana, on ceremonial occasions, wore "their" jewels. This is another instance of that unusual bond between ruler and ruled, *raja* and *praja*, who are deemed to be members of one family.

Maharana Lakha Singh likewise developed the zinc and silver mines which were to remain an important source of revenue to the State for the next five hundred years (and are still mined by the Indian government today). Finally, Lakha's patronage of the arts laid the foundation for that long tradition of Mewar painting about which we shall hear more in subsequent generations.

When Maharana Lakha was an old man, his eldest son and heir, Chunda, was due to be married to a daughter of the neighbouring royal house of Marwar. In accordance with custom, the envoy from Marwar came bearing a coconut (the symbol of marriage) which he intended to present to Chunda. Chunda, however, was not at court on the day in question, so his father the Maharana accepted the coconut on his behalf, with the light-hearted remark that doubtless no princess would want to accept an old fellow in his dotage, so there was little risk of making a mistake! When Chunda was informed of this repartee, he was outraged. In Tod's elegant phrase, he was "offended at delicacy being sacrificed to wit" and he declined to accept the symbol. In truth, he was subjecting Hindu scripture to absurdly literal interpretation, holding that the thought of a wrong thing was a sin in itself. Chunda might have been a shade too solemn!

He certainly placed his father in a very embarrassing position. Conscious that the symbol could not be returned without gross insult to the princess and her family, Maharana Lakha Singh took the only way out; he was obliged to turn his jest to serious account by marrying the girl himself. He made the condition that Chunda should renounce his right to the *gadi* of Mewar in favour of any issue of this new marriage. As far as we know, Chunda readily assented, and was even pleased when a baby boy was born. He thereupon left Chittor in good humour and with good grace, while his little half-brother, Mokal, assumed the role of heir. It is only the second time in the long history of this family that the mantle of Maharana had fallen upon the younger, not the older, son. (The third instance occurs in our own day.) Chunda's descendants even now talk of his sacrifice with pride.

When Maharana Lakha died, Mokal was still an infant, so the governance of the State passed to a regent, the Queen's nephew Jodha, prince of the House of Marwar. To avert the danger of Mewar passing into foreign hands by stealth, Chunda reclaimed his father's right to Chittor on behalf of his brother Mokal, and Jodha retired to his own State of Marwar, where he founded the city of Jodhpur, named after him, and unwittingly gave his name also to an enduring fashion of riding-breeches made popular in the West ("jodhpurs").

Mokal succeeded as Maharana Mokal Singh and ruled from 1421 to 1433. Most evidence of his reign has been obliterated, but there is one fine temple, intact, which the visitor sees in front of the Tower of Victory at Chittor and often neglects. This splendid building still retains the capacity to speak to us across the centuries and rescues Mokal from being a mere name in the sequence. His major contribution to the family history was, however, to be father of one of the greatest Maharanas of them all—Kumbha, and he also renovated the Shree Eklingnath ji Temple at Kailashpuri.

When we come to this man we enter upon another period of heroism, for Kumbha was one of the great military generals of the Sisodia clan. But there is much more than that, and the ripples of his gigantic achievements may still be felt today by anyone with an imaginative disposition. Kumbha was a ruler of such varied talents that he rivalled the Italian Renaissance ideal of *l'uomo universale*, of the man adept in music and literature as well as on the battlefield. As a patron, he reminds one of Lorenzo de' Medici.

Kumbha reigned for over thirty years, from 1433 to 1468, during which time the stability initiated by his grandfather Lakha was consolidated by a burst of creative energy which made Chittor a centre of culture for the whole continent. This was not achieved, however, without some struggle; how to meet challenges of every variety honed those emergent characteristics of the Mewar dynasty which were to distinguish them from any other.

First, it must be recalled that, by virtue of the resistance of Ratan, Hamir, Lakha and Mokal, Mewar had been isolated as a Hindu kingdom. Other Rajput states had succumbed, and both the neighbouring states of Gujarat and Malwa were under the sway of powerful Muslim Sultans, who had won independence from the central authority of Delhi and were themselves anxious for expansion. Mewar was invaded several times and vigorously defended by Maharana Kumbha. In 1437 Mahmud, the King of Malwa, made another attempt. He was captured and taken prisoner to Chittor after a vicious and heavy battle. Notwithstanding the fact that he was a Muslim, and an admitted enemy, Rana Kumbha treated him as a guest for six months, and when finally Mahmud was released, he went home not only without demands for ransom, but also bearing gifts from his captor. As we shall see time and again, magnanimity of this kind was to be a hallmark of Mewari conduct in victory.

Which is not to say, of course, that the people must be denied their celebration, this being perfectly compatible with generosity towards the foe. Maharana Kumbha built a triumphal column at Chittor, 120 feet high and rising through nine storeys, known as the Tower of Victory. It took ten years to complete, and, five hundred years later, it is as impressive now as it must have been then. The Vijai Stambh (to give it its proper name) is now recognised as one of the most important monuments in India, not only historically, but architecturally. First, it owes nothing to Muslim influence, but is a pure example of Hindu style and craftsmanship. Second, it offers eloquent testimony to Hindu tolerance and cultural Catholicism, for not only is the Tower an illustrated history of Hindu mythology, which can be "read" by the curious scholar, but also a record of every other religion in India, each being represented by its own symbol (amazingly, the word "Allah" in Arabic inscription can still be discerned). It will be well to bear in mind the significance of this Tower and its message as we continue our journey through the family history. The message is simple but rare: that human dignity cannot be enhanced by religious antagonism or bigotry, but only reviled, disgraced. The corollary of this is that the enemy is not Muslim, or Christian, or even pagan, but he alone who threatens freedom, whatever he be.

The Tower of Victory at Chittor was by no means the only building erected by Maharana Kumbha, though time has determined it should be the most illustrious. It provides also, incidentally, one of the rare instances where the names of the architects have been discovered—Sutdrahar Jaita and his three sons, Napa, Puja and Poma. Kumbha was a relentless builder, constructing no less than thirty-two of the eighty-four fortresses in Mewar, including the monumental fort named after him—Kumbhalgarh. Two hours north of Udaipur on the road that passes through Ekling ji, Kumbhalgarh is a sight to make one stumble. As one turns the corner and first catches sight of those grand undulating walls high, high on a hill where it was inconceivable anyone should even dare to think of construction, one is so surprised it might almost be termed a shock, akin to one's first gawping view of the Grand Canyon in Arizona. Thirty-three kilometres of walls, over twenty feet thick, encircle the hill, on the very summit of which is the palace itself, a majestic undertaking.

In Chittor, Maharana Kumbha was responsible for the palace which bears his name and which, in its noble ruins, holds his spirit. The domestic rooms are still visible, as is the circular elephant stable, with its central post to which the elephant was tethered. The jagged outline of the ruins etched against the sky may often nowadays be adorned with the profiles of monkeys, who have made Kumbha's palace their home. Kumbha also built numerous residences, temples, streets, all of which were enclosed within the city walls, not, as today, scattered without. He also established important schools of art and architecture, giving patronage to eighteen separate classes of artisans living and working under his protection. The range and skill of Hindu craftsmen, especially stonemasons, which would one day be of considerable benefit to the Moghul emperors, were due in no small measure to the atmosphere of cultural enterprise and experiment encouraged by Rana Kumbha. Literature and music likewise flourished. Indeed, it would hardly be an exaggeration to say that Chittor, under Kumbha, became the Florence of north-west India.

As for Kumbha's own contribution to the arts, it is difficult after such a passage of time to evaluate how much should be ascribed to genius and how much to patronage. He is credited with having written four dramas in Sanskrit, many poems, a justly famous book on genealogy, a study of the Tower of Victory and its purpose, books of literary criticism and judgement, as well as pages of musical composition which are sung to this day. Much of his vast output was undoubtedly his, but it is fair to suggest that some may have been the work of scholars and artists working under his roof or in collaboration with him. "School of Kumbha" is often a safer assignation than anything else. Many of the famous books on sculpture were written by Mandan, Nath or Govind. Nonetheless, the plays and the music are definitely by Maharana Kumbha, who was an erudite man, an authority on grammar, deeply learned and personally accomplished, as keen on the development of artistic excellence as any Medici. The cultural life of Mewar was never higher than under his rule, and there are many who would accord him the highest accolade as the best king the state ever had.

History being the record of human transgression as well as achievement, it is rarely just in its distribution of fate. The great and good Kumbha was assassinated by his eldest son who, as a consequence, is hardly mentioned in the family chronicles and has been relegated to the shadows of non-existence with a remorselessness any modern Communist historian might match. The murder took place in the extant temple at Kumbhalgarh, and the perpetrator is merely referred to as "the murderer". Five years later, his brother succeeded as Maharana Raimal, of whom little is known save that he installed the present idol of Ekling ji. In the next generation, the 50th, another giant among men ascends the *gadi* of Mewar—Maharana Sangram Singh (1509–1527), known to his people from that day to this as simply "Rana Sanga", and to the chroniclers as "Mighty Sanga".

Mewar reached the apex of its prosperity under Sanga, if only because the hiatus in power at Delhi, and the demoralisation of the rest of Rajputana left Chittor, not for the first time, nor the last, the sole defender of Hinduism in northern India. For a time, there was even the possibility that Sanga might compete with Delhi to bring stability to a land far more extensive than Mewar itself, and he did extend his influence, though his race had never been interested in conquest as such. His entire reign was consumed with defensive battles, of which there were so many that Sanga himself lost an arm and an eye, was crippled in one leg, and suffered eighty-four wounds to his body. When in 1519 the Sultan of

Mandu was taken prisoner and lodged at Chittor, there occurred a repetition of the generosity displayed by Maharana Kumbha; Sanga not only tended his Muslim enemy's wounds and waited upon him as his personal guest, but released him and even restored him to the kingdom which he could so easily have annexed.

Sanga was loyal to the strict Rajput code of chivalry, which determined that selflessness should be honoured not only in reckless personal bravery, but in respect for the weak and proper behaviour towards a defeated enemy. Again, it is not fanciful to see in this code a parallel with the ideals of Renaissance Europe, which found expression in the wisdom of the great French writer Rabelais. In his *Gargantua*, Book XIX, his victorious hero Grandgousier says, "*Ma deliberation n'est de provocquer, ains d'apaiser; d'assailir, mais defendre; de conquester, mais de guarder mes feaulx subjectz et terres hereditaires.*" ("My purpose is not to provoke, but to appease; not to attack, but to defend; not to conquer, but to protect my faithful subjects and hereditary lands.") Emotionally, if not entirely accurately, Sanga is regarded as the last Hindu emperor of India. It was his misfortune that he lived long enough to witness the arrival of the Moghuls, whose principles were as far removed from those of Rabelais as it is possible to imagine. They were destined to subjugate India for the next two hundred years and burden the State of Mewar with its most arduous sufferings yet.

The Sultans held sway in Delhi from 1206 to 1526, when they were overthrown by the first of the Moghuls, Babur. The Moghuls were of mixed stock, including Mongolian, and of Muslim faith. Mercifully, however, at least until their final demise under the dreadful Aurangzeb, they did not share the fanatical bigotry of their predecessors, the Sultans, but were closer to the Rajputs in their encouragement of religious harmony. Babur himself was a notable poet and diarist, his autobiography being counted among the masterpieces of oriental literature. None of this, however, mitigated in any degree his zeal for conquest, and he found his ambitions easy to attain except when thwarted by the obstinacy of the Rajputs, united for once in their history under the leadership of Maharana Sanga.

Sanga's forces halted the advance of Babur at the battle of Khanua in 1527, which they showed every sign of winning until Sanga was deserted by one of his generals who made a treacherous alliance with the enemy. Sanga was struck by an arrow and had to be carried unconscious from the field. He retreated to Baswa near Bharatpur, where he died later that year, possibly poisoned.

Sanga had four sons, three of whom succeeded to the *gadi* in turn, Maharana Ratan Singh reigned only four years, from 1527 to 1531, and was followed by his brother Vikramaditya, a passionately argumentative man who found it difficult to secure agreement among his nobles. It was during his time that the second of the three sacks of Chittor took place, in 1535, when forces from Gujarat, supported by Portuguese mercenaries with modern weaponry, unexpectedly attacked.

Sanga's widow, Karnavati, led all her womenfolk into Chittor's second act of *johar*, mass suicide, though accounts differ as to how exactly this was effected. Was it a traditional funeral pyre? Or was there insufficient time to construct one, and they had consequently to blow themselves up with gunpowder? The funeral pyre sounds much more convincing, according as it does with sacred custom.

At any rate, the skies glowed with the fire of their immolation when the city was once more devastated by a ruthless foe. Thirty-two thousand Rajput warriors charged into enemy lines "in blind and impatient despair", certain that they would all be slaughtered. They carried into death the Mewar banner of a golden sun and black peacock feathers.

Vikramaditya had escaped in the meantime, returning to find not only a ruined city, but equally ruinous conflict among what was left of the family. The heir, his brother Udai, was only six years old. His distant kinsman, a bastard offspring called Banveer, had assumed control as regent and quickly made it clear that he aimed even higher. He assassinated Vikramaditiya and then turned his attentions to the only obstacle to his progress, the sole surviving direct descendant of Bappa Rawal—young Udai.

The boy's nurse, Panna Dhai, had taken on the duties of foster-mother after the death of his own mother in the mass suicide of 1535, and protected him with exemplary devotion. Their living quarters were high up in a corner of Kumbha's Palace at Chittor, and the room may still be made out among the ruins. Panna Dhai heard screams coming from the *zenana* (that portion of the palace reserved for the ladies), and realised that the insatiable Banveer was hunting for Udai. She quickly placed the infant in a fruit basket, covered him with leaves, and entrusted a manservant to smuggle him to safety. She then substituted her own child in the cot, and when Banveer arrived in a frenzy of power-lust, he plunged his sword into the bundle and killed the child outright. The tiny corpse was immediately burned on a pyre before Panna, weeping, made her escape from Chittor to join the heir and the servant.

It seems Panna did not easily find refuge. The preciousness of her charge and the political danger of offering protection to him while the merciless Banveer held the reins of power, frightened off a number of royal houses who ought to have opened their doors to the brave woman. For weeks, perhaps months, she wandered the country trying to conceal her identity from the fearful and reveal it only to those who appeared loyal subjects. Eventually, she found sanctuary in the fort at Kumbhalgarh, where Udai was raised as nephew to the fort's Governor, little suspecting the destiny that awaited him. By the time he was thirteen, however, the noblemen of Mewar recognised him as their king and invested him at Kumbhalgarh as Maharana Udai Singh, 53rd of the line. He had been *de jure* monarch since 1537, but did not assume the dignity and duties of Maharana until 1542.

The selfless Panna Dhai has been honoured from that day as a heroine of the Sisodia clan, revered alike for her loyalty and swift action. For those of us who visit Udaipur today and look back on the history of the family, Panna is one of the most significant figures in the story. For, without her intervention, the city of Udaipur would never have existed.

Maharana Pratap attacking Man Singh of Jaipur in the battle of Haldi Ghati, 1576
Attributed to artists Raghunath and Damodar
Acc. No. 2011.26.0013

THE FOUNDATION OF UDAIPUR
AND THE GLORY OF PRATAP

Istory has been unnecessarily harsh in its assessment of Udai Singh; more than that even, its judgement has probably been a cruel travesty. Taking her cue from Tod, Sylvia Matheson Muller stated baldly that "unfortunately, Udai was not cast in the heroic mould of his ancestors." When the third and final attack on Chittor was made in 1567 by the greatest of Moghul emperors, the formidable Akbar, Maharana Udai Singh is said to have fled the city and sought refuge rather than face his daunting duty. Perhaps the bardic chroniclers wanted to render the glory of his son and successor, Pratap, all the more blinding by means of a neat contrast. If so, Colonel Tod cast aside all critical doubt and accepted a biased version of events, leaving to posterity a damning portrait of a weak, pusillanimous man, "a coward succeeding a bastard to guide the destinies of the Sisodias." This is what Tod wrote:

> Udai Singh had not one quality of a sovereign; and wanting martial virtue, the common heritage of his race, he was destitute of all. Yet he might have slumbered his life away in inglorious repose during the reign of Humayun [successor to Emperor Babur in Delhi]; but, unhappily for Rajasthan, a prince was then rearing who forged fetters for the Hindu race which enthralled them for ages [Akbar].

Tod goes on to claim that the Maharana abandoned Chittor under attack, leaving his wives and noblemen to cope without him, and more or less ran for the hills. "The absence of the kingly virtues in the sovereign of Mewar filled to the brim the bitter cup of her destiny." The truth is much more subtle than this.

The second sack of Chittor, in 1535, was still within recent memory, and that devastating blow had laid waste the achievements of two hundred years—both the cultural legacy of Maharana Kumbha and the military and political advances of Maharana Sanga. When Maharana Udai Singh was invested at Kumbhalgarh he was still a boy and the misery of his people only five years before yet echoed in his ears. He was likely to yearn to avenge, but unlikely to want a repetition of disaster. It was becoming more and more obvious that the mighty fortress was no longer impregnable against the onslaught of modern warfare. That it stood high and isolated in the middle of a flat plain, as one writer has put it, "like a coronet on the surface of the earth", destitute of any natural defences, open to all sides, meant that it was almost certain not to survive another sophisticated attack, and that yet another display of mad bravery and mass suicide would be inevitable. Who could tell how long such insecurity might continue? By the time he was a mature man in his thirties, Udai Singh realised the futility of ignoring changed circumstances and made a pragmatic, strategic, and ultimately wise decision. He began to look for a safer place at which to construct a new capital.

Returning to the Aravalli hills, which had been the cradle of his ancestors one thousand years before, the Maharana recognised the sense of building in a valley with the protection of hills, forests, and lakes around. There was already a fine lake, Pichola, at the head of which was a lofty hill. In the forest, Udai Singh encountered an ascetic, an old man who had renounced all worldly things and who was therefore beyond caste. He advised him to establish a settlement at the end of the lake and to enlarge the lake itself. Thus were laid the first stones of the city of Udaipur (which Udai named after himself) in 1559. This was some eight years before the final attack on Chittor by Emperor Akbar. To this day, at the shrine in the very heart of the City Palace at Udaipur, known as the Dhuni Mata, burns a flame in perpetual gratitude to the ascetic who gave Udai his resolve. It marks the oldest part of the palace, and the most sensible point at which to begin a view of the rambling additions which have encrusted around it.

Udai Singh had therefore already begun the establishment of a new centre on the shores of Lake Pichola before the final attack on Chittor in 1567 (between 1559 and 1564, while the palace was under construction, he lived briefly on the shores of another nearby lake, the Udai Sagar). Far from taking flight from the fortress in the midst of battle, he had foreseen the hopelessness of Chittor's plight and determined that the best way of ensuring the survival of his race and monarchy was to take measures for the total removal of his seat of authority to a land protected by valleys and defiles, rather than place reliance on the old system of forts and ramparts. He was, in other words, a modern, forward-looking *homme politique.* Only the very old and the very young were left in Mewar, a whole generation of men having been wiped out in the siege of 1535. The Sisodia clan was exhausted, almost to the point of extinction, by the struggles of protracted war. Udai Singh gave himself time and space to reorganise, and in the meantime made the land around Chittor inhospitable to any invading army and constantly harassed potential supply lines. This was an example of the guerrilla tactics later to be refined and made supremely effective by his son, the great hero Pratap.

Akbar moved against Chittor precisely because it symbolised Rajput resistance and was the most famous jewel of Rajput civilisation in the land. He knew that if he could subdue the Sisodias, the lesser Rajput clans would be so intimidated they would capitulate the more easily. Maharana Udai Singh was determined Akbar should be denied this satisfaction.

Akbar's attack on Chittor was fiercely opposed by the entire population, led by two Rajput warriors, Jaimal and Patta, each only sixteen years old. Both they and their beloved city were doomed, but their courage was by no means diminished by the certainty of defeat. Patta had recently been married; his wife and mother armed themselves with lances and joined the headlong rush down the cliff to meet their foe. Both Jaimal and Patta perished in the battle, and are today sung as heroes of Mewar.

There followed the final act of *johar.* The funeral pyre consumed nine queens, five princesses, the families and children of all the noblemen left in Chittor. Beneath the surface of the ground which lies between the Tower of Victory and Mokal's Temple there is a layer of (presumably human) ashes which betokens the final collapse. Thirty thousand inhabitants of the fort, including seventeen hundred of the ruler's kinsmen, died on this occasion. Even girls of fifteen went out fighting or went into the fire. "It is awe-inspiring to think of it," wrote Charles Allen.

That was the end of Chittor. Akbar, a paradoxical man, responded with two contrasting gestures. He vengefully and wantonly did his utmost to destroy all remaining works of art in the once-flourishing centre of culture, and he erected statues in memory of the brave youths, Jaimal and Patta, at the gates of his fort at Delhi. His admiration for their courage matched his frustration at their success. It is not without significance, also, that Maharana Udai Singh refused to swear allegiance to Akbar, in contrast with the rulers of Jodhpur, Bikaner and Jaisalmer, who all bowed in subservience, and it is only fair, in the light of his subsequent reputation, that such fortitude be recorded.

Though Chittor was gone, the spirit of the Sisodia clan did not go with it. Udai Singh died in 1572. To please his favourite queen, Bhatiyani, he had stipulated that her son, Jagmal, the second-born of his twenty-five male offspring, should succeed him in defiance of all custom and precedence. (They, of course, had repaired to the new settlement at Udaipur and not been among the casualties.) But no sooner did Jagmal make his way to the *gadi* than two noblemen took him by the arm (one hopes gently), affirming, "You have made a mistake, Maharaj. That place belongs to your brother." Thus did the greatest of all Mewari patriots, Pratap, take his throne on a stone (at a village called Gogunda), since when all Maharanas have been invested in this way instead of on the more usual cushion, favoured by other Rajput rulers.

For a Westerner, already confused by the unfamiliarity of Hindu names and bewildered by the richness of a history of which he may well have heard nothing, it helps to seek parallels in European life in order to create some kind of recognisable measure. If Rana Kumbha was the Lorenzo de' Medici of the Sisodia dynasty, and Rana Sanga the Duke of Wellington, Rana Pratap most resembles, in his dogged perseverance against paralysing odds and blunt refusal ever to give in, Winston Churchill in 1940. It is crucial to remember that he was the ruler of a land whose ancient capital was in foreign hands, as Churchill came close to being at the beginning of the Second World War. Like Churchill, he could promise his people nothing but "blood, sweat and tears". His was the one tiny pool of resistance in what had become the vast ocean of the Moghul Empire, and his obstinate defence of freedom became, and has remained, an inspiration not only to Mewar and Udaipur, but to the whole of India.

The famous battle of Haldi Ghati took place on 18 June, 1576. Tod called it the Thermopylae of Mewar history, but it deserves to be remembered perhaps, not so much for its strategy and courage as for its cause. Haldi Ghati was fought for a principle, which Akbar tried to break and Pratap would not yield.

Mewar was encircled and blockaded by Akbar's allies, Rajput princes who had sold out to the emperor's demands; they included the rulers of Marwar, Amber, Bikaner, and Bundi. The confederation of Rajput states established by Sanga had totally disintegrated. To be fair, the allies had not become slaves or servants to Akbar, and from one point of view Pratap's pride was excessive. Akbar respected the internal sovereignty of states which signalled their allegiance. He never attempted to interfere with their culture, for which, indeed, he nursed a lively admiration. They surrendered control only of their foreign policy, and their allegiance was solely to the ideal of an ultimate suzerainty. Akbar could not allow his concept of nationhood to be subverted by a hero, and an exception in Pratap's favour would have set a bad example to the others. The issue turned, therefore, on whether Pratap would appear at the Moghul court in token recognition of Akbar's status as emperor. Akbar would not compromise on this one point, and Pratap would not satisfy him. That was the principle over which the battle was fought. As Vincent Smith wrote, "Pratap's patriotism was his offence."

The other important characteristic of this battle is its secular nature. In no sense at all was it a conflict flamed by religious strife. Akbar was a tolerant man, respectful of the religious convictions of others. Islamic Jihad, or "holy war", was no part of his purpose. The leader of his forces was in fact a Rajput, Raja Man Singh of Amber, while the leader of Pratap's forces was a Pathan, Hakim Khan Sur. With a Hindu at the head of the Muslims and a Muslim at the head of the Hindus, it would be foolish to see the contest as one fought for narrow ideological gain. For Pratap, freedom was not divisible.

Akbar had earlier sent envoys to Pratap to seek his submission. They were repulsed with courtesy. The siege which followed led to the heroic battle itself. Pratap tried once to sue for peace before resorting to battle; in his turn, he sent envoys proposing that Akbar should lift the siege and Pratap would make reasonable compensation. In other words, Akbar should name his price. The emperor laughed at this, saying, "I am not a plunderer, but a conqueror!" and made it clear that nothing less than Pratap's surrender would assuage him. The envoys refused. So impressed was he by their reckless bravery (for he assumed they knew they would be slaughtered by his superior army), as well as by the code of honour which drove them, that he asked what he could do for them. They replied that if they died in battle, Akbar should grant them a Hindu cremation. He promised that he would.

The battle itself is of interest to the student of military strategy, as it was fought in a narrow pass in the mountains ("Haldi Ghati") which precluded any massed strength. Mounted on his white stallion, Chetak, Pratap plunged headlong into Akbar's troops with a speed which appeared manic, and took them so by surprise that they scattered. He made straight for Man Singh, mounted on an elephant. The horse Chetak reared up in front of the elephant and struck it on the head with its front leg; the driver of the elephant was killed by Pratap, but Man Singh escaped with his life by crouching in the *howdah*. The elephant fled in panic, but it had, in the encounter with Chetak, almost severed the horse's leg with the sword it carried in its trunk (this is not the stuff of legend—elephants were trained to wield swords in battle). With his mount wounded, Pratap was forced to retire, while the Jhala chief took over leadership and gave his life in a wild sortie into enemy lines, giving

Pratap time to retreat to the hills. The wounded Chetak climbed up over rocks, wracked with pain, bearing his exhausted master on his back, until he reached a secluded place of safety. His mission accomplished, he then dropped dead at his master's feet.

The horse is remembered with pride as one of the heroes of Haldi Ghati, and a small *chhatri* (stone pavilion) marks the spot where he died. Another was Hakim Khan Sur who fought so zealously, it is said, that his sword could not be detached from his hand, and he was buried (as a Muslim) clutching it even in death. Haldi Ghati itself is a place of pilgrimage for thousands, who reverently pick up the yellow sand of the pass and wipe it on their foreheads in homage to the defender of their rights.

Was it a victory for Pratap? His men melted away into the hills and could not be tracked down. Pratap himself evaded capture. Akbar's army, on the other hand, was at his mercy. Pratap controlled Akbar's supply lines, and with his knowledge of the hills and the intelligence network of his Bhil tribesmen, who reported every movement, he was able to prevent the Imperial army from receiving any provisions. They were reduced to starvation, and to eating their own horses. They were blocked at all exits. Pratap, living rough in the hills and undergoing many personal hardships, his children cradled in baskets hung from the trees, became master of what has come to be known as "guerilla warfare". With policies of scorched earth and harassment, and by being constantly on the move, he contrived to remain an irritant to the ambitions of Akbar, who was eventually compelled to give up. Mao Tse-tung wrote that "guerillas do not win wars, but their enemies do lose them." By this reckoning, Pratap was trimphant, despite the fact of his retreat. As Kesri Singh has written, "For the Imperial army, no victory was ever more like defeat; for Mewar, no retreat more glorious."

There was no escaping the major significance for the Moghuls, namely that in their plans to overpower the Rajputs they had suffered their first setback in fifty years. Haldi Ghati shattered the myth of their invincibility.

For the last ten years of his life, Maharana Pratap was able to rule without any further interference. Single-handedly, he had maintained the independence of his country with tiny forces, and in the end regained almost the whole of the hereditary State of Mewar.

He was clearly a charismatic personality. In appearance he was noble and striking, with those uncommonly large eyes which he inherited from Maharana Kumbha and which have ever been a feature of the Sisodia dynasty. They seemed to suggest a fire and determination within. Like Churchill, he drove himself and his men hard, not brooking any sign of faintheartedness, and ever alert to the threat of humiliation. On the other hand, he was fair and benign; realising that summary or arbitrary justice might alienate his men, he instituted a system wherein guilt was dependent upon evidence, and the accused were innocent in the absence of proof. Consequently, his court was free of that intrigue and bartering for influence which thwart and defile many a noble purpose.

When Pratap died in 1597, an extraordinary thing happened. The Emperor Akbar cried. The court poet recited a verse in Pratap's honour, which in translation begins, "Guhilot Rana, you have won even in death, because on hearing of your demise the emperor was silent, bit his tongue, sighed, and tears welled up in his eyes. You had not allowed your horses to be branded, nor bowed your head before anyone." The assembled courtiers trembled at the poet's temerity, expecting him to be punished. Instead, Akbar rewarded him. This, by the way, is a Muslim historian's account of what happened.

Plays and poems were written to celebrate Pratap's glory, and countless thousands of children have been named after him in the course of the ensuing four centuries. The famous vows he made during the period of his greatest trial, when Kumbhalgarh, Chittor, and the incipient Udaipur were all occupied by Moghul forces and he was being hunted from one valley to the next, have been repeated in each generation. They are, that no Maharana would ever offer obeisance to Delhi as long as India remained under foreign yolk, nor even deign to be summoned to Delhi lest such be interpreted as submission; and that, in recognition of fortune's whimsical habits, every Maharana would eat off a plate of leaves and sleep on a bed of grass, as he had done in the forest. Even today, the head of the family will place leaves beneath his plate and grass under his bed on certain days of the year in token respect to the vow of Pratap and the humility of his example.

Pratap's name has been immortalised far beyond the confines of Mewar, in books and poems written in such diverse tongues as Sanskrit, Rajasthani, Hindi and Gujarati, as well as English. As the first freedom fighter in the annals of India, he was the precursor and inspiration of Mahatma Gandhi himself. To the people at large, he is known forever as "the Light and Life of the Hindu community".

THE PERIOD OF CONSTRUCTION
MAHARANA JAGAT SINGH

Pratap had seventeen sons, of whom the eldest, Amar, succeeded him as Maharana Amar Singh I (1597–1620). The Emperor Akbar was still alive and no less anxious to achieve the homogeneity of his empire, which Udaipur alone stubbornly resisted. It is only fair to point out that Akbar was not merely a conqueror, but an idealist, with a deep and honourable desire to bring a civilising influence to bear upon India. He dreamed of one whole united country ruled by a benevolent imperialism, and even hoped he would be able to synthesise two such disparate cultures as the Hindu and the Muslim. His fascination with metaphysics and philosophy led him to believe that such an ambition was capable of realisation, but he had first to secure the alliance of the recalcitrant and proud Sisodias. To this end, he treated Amar Singh with scrupulous courtesy, making clear his admiration for Amar's father, his old adversary Pratap. For eight years, Udaipur was left in peace.

Akbar was succeeded as emperor by his son Jahangir, a man far less endowed with either patience or intellect. He renewed the war with Udaipur, launching seventeen pitched battles over the next ten years, until finally Amar Singh was worn down and forced to negotiate a peace. He nevertheless secured especial exemption for himself and his successors from personal attendance at the Moghul court, in honour of his father's pledge (which, of course, his people would never have forgiven him for betraying). His son would represent him. As a consequence of this compromise, only heirs have been to Delhi, and no Maharana has attended *qua* Maharana. Another part of the peace restored Chittor to the Maharana on condition he did not fortify or repair the city.

Despite such reasonable terms, Amar Singh was so dejected by the implicit submission they concealed, that he never again emerged from the privacy of his palace.

Amar Singh was succeeded by Maharana Karan Singh (1620–1628) who, enjoying a reign which was blessed by the peace his father had arranged, was able to devote his energies to the improvement of his palace and its surroundings. He is one of the great builders of the line, responsible for many of the rooms, courtyards and halls in the City Palace which we see today; indeed, he was the first really to have the leisure to indulge such intent, as Pratap had

Jagmandir, Lake Pichola, Udaipur (also known as the Lake Garden Palace)
An island palace at the southern end of Lake Pichola, Udaipur, completed and named by Maharana Jagat Singh I (1628–1652)
Print designed by H. Clerget; Photograph by M.L. Rousselet
Acc. No. 2011.T.0019

more or less bankrupted the State with his wars, and Amar was constantly on the defensive. Karan Singh constructed most of the *zenana mahal* (women's quarters), just inside the main entrance. He also fortified Udaipur's city walls, strengthened the dam which encloses Lake Pichola, and began construction of the delightful little pleasure palace sitting peacefully in the middle of the lake, called Jagmandir. From the heights of Shiv Niwas Palace, looking across the lake to the Aravalli hills, it is the quiet, untroubled island on the left, now a haven for hundreds of species of exotic birds.

Jagmandir holds its own especial place in the family history for being the scene of a quite remarkable instance of unreserved hospitality. The son of Emperor Jahangir, Prince Khurram, instigated a rebellion against his father, for which transgression he was banished into exile. Amazingly, he sought refuge with the Moghuls' hereditary enemy, the Maharana of Udaipur, and his request was granted. Karan Singh housed the prince at Jagmandir (then still uncompleted), probably for a few months, though historians differ as to exactly how long his residence lasted.

One thing is certain, when Emperor Jahangir died in 1627 and Prince Khurram succeeded as Emperor Shah Jahan, he was still lodged at Jagmandir, so that his proclamation was announced from Udaipur, and the tributary princes of the Moghul Empire came there to acknowledge his accession. There can be no better tribute to the tolerant ideals of Kumbha and Sanga—that distress should be alleviated irrespective of religion or enmity, and no surer proof that those ideals would be upheld. Further opportunities for their expression would be presented, and grasped, in the centuries to come.

In token of affection and respect, the Maharana and the emperor exchanged turbans at the latter's departure from Udaipur, each placing his own on the other's head. Shah Jahan's turban, still in the folds it held that day, is now in the government museum at the City Palace. It was even said that when he built the Taj Mahal, Shah Jahan was inspired by his memories of Jagmandir.

One year later, in 1628, Jagat Singh I ascended the *gadi* of Udaipur and ruled for twenty-four years of prosperity and calm, "exchanging the din of arms for voluptuous inactivity", to borrow Tod's pious expression. Never mind; he used it to good effect. He is justly credited with being one of the great architects of the dynasty, and is responsible for the beautiful island of Jagmandir, to which he gave his name.

Jagat Singh likewise made further additions to the City Palace, growing now with each generation like a coral expanding ever upwards and outwards. Palaces were built on top of other palaces, or tacked on to their sides, the rocky hill beneath them being continually tamed to provide foundations where none might have been thought possible. When the hill ran out of space, vast buttresses were formed to extend it artificially, with the result that, if one were able to view the mile-long palace from the lake with an X-ray lens, one would see the jagged outline of the hill rising up within it. Some courtyards at the very top, sprinkled with trees and shrubs, appear to be on the roof, but in fact are at ground level, since the ground rises to that height and there are no rooms beneath. To the visitor, this is all very confusing and disorienting, and we shall consider in its proper place the style and function of this bewildering edifice. For the moment, it is enough to say that the whole construction is a marvel of architectural skill, which we owe to the vision of successive Maharanas and their artisans. It is bootless to attempt to say who exactly built the City Palace, as no less than twenty-two Maharanas have added to it and left their mark upon it (the sole exception being the soldier Pratap), but it is fair to suggest that Jagat Singh was one of the most prolific builders along with his father Karan Singh.

Not only that. He was also a serious patron of the arts, resurrecting the cultural traditions of his great ancestor Kumbha. The reader who is anxious to explore further the legacy of the Mewar School of Painting should consult those experts like Andrew Topsfield and G.N. Sharma who have traced its history with care. In Topsfield's words, "the fortunes of a Rajput kingdom are chiefly dependent upon the character of its ruler. In the long history of court painting at Udaipur the interest and discrimination of individual Maharanas did most to determine the quality of artistic work produced for them."

Jagat Singh's principal artist was Sahibdin, who carried forward the tradition of religious manuscript painting inherited by the Rajputs, and overlaid it with some Moghul influence. In the later reigns of Raj Singh I (1653–1680), Jai Singh (1680–1698), and Amar Singh II (1698–1710), court painting continued to flourish, and Topsfield affirms that it reached its highest point of perfection under the latter—Maharana Amar Singh II. The intricacy of these paintings, executed in miniature with the finest brush taken from the throat of a squirrel and often only one delicate hair in thickness, have to be seen to be believed. Some have found their way to museums in Mumbai and the West, especially at Adelaide in Australia, but many remain on the walls of the City Palace, and some at Shiv Niwas and the Fateh Prakash Palace.

Further engineering feats were undertaken at the same time. Against the background of the most terrifying drought and pestilence known in the seventeenth century, Maharana Raj Singh built the lake known as Rajsamand, to save his people from famine. Just how dangerous can be these droughts which from time to time are inflicted upon Rajasthan is made clear by an all-too-vivid contemporary account which deserves substantial quotation:

> For want of water the world was in despair, and people went mad with hunger. Things unknown as food were eaten. The husband abandoned the wife, the wife the husband; parents sold their children; time increased the evil; it spread far and wide. Even the insects died, they had nothing to feed on. Thousands of all ages became victims to hunger. Those who procured food today ate twice what nature required. The wind was from the west, a pestilential vapour. The constellations were always visible at night, nor was there a cloud in the sky by day, and thunder and lightning were unknown. Such portents filled mankind with dread. Rivers, lakes and fountains were dried up. Men of wealth meted out the portions of food; the ministers of religion forgot their duties. There was no longer distinction of caste, and the

Sudra and Brahmin were undistinguishable. Strength, wisdom, caste, tribe, all were abandoned, and food alone was the object. All was lost in hunger. Fruits, flowers, every vegetable thing, even trees were stripped of their bark, to appease the cravings of hunger; nay, *man ate man*! Cities were depopulated. The seed of families was lost, the fishes were extinct, and the hope of all extinguished.

The construction of lake Rajsamand was intended to ensure that nothing like this should ever occur again.

Some nineteenth-century accounts say that Raj Singh murdered his eldest son, but this story has disappeared as mysteriously as it erupted—Tod did not so much as mention it. In the next generation, Maharana Jai Singh dammed a pass in the mountains thirty miles south of Udaipur to construct the magnificent lake of Jaisamund, which remained, until the building of the Aswan dam in Egypt, the largest artificial lake in the world.

Meanwhile, the political scene again exploded into turbulence. To understand the origin of this fresh outbreak of violence we must return to the death of Maharana Jagat Singh in 1652 and the succession of his son Raj Singh. It was in his reign that the reasonable Shah Jahan died, and the mantle of emperor passed to Aurangzeb, the most bigoted, fanatic, and frankly the nastiest, of all the Moghuls. For many years Raj Singh was locked in fierce conflict with this unrelenting man, who was bent upon another "holy" war for the elimination of Hinduism, and who persecuted the State of Mewar with remorseless vigour. The Maharana, it need hardly be said, was equally as determined to protect the interests of his people.

Aurangzeb imposed a crippling tax on the people of Mewar which, following the devastating drought, imposed a burden they could not be expected to endure. Raj Singh wrote to the emperor, appealing vainly in the name of his father Shah Jahan. "The tribute you demand from the Hindus is repugnant to justice", he said. "It is equally foreign from good policy as it must impoverish the country." His eloquence went unheeded.

Aurangzeb's arrogance was punctured on another front. He made it known that he intended to take as wife the Princess Charumathi, from Rathore family of Kishangarh State. The proposal was, to her, insulting, and she besought Maharana Raj Singh to rescue her from a cruel future. This he did by marrying her himself, and the emperor was predictably furious when he learnt of such wilful obstruction.

Lastly, he went so far as to declare the shrine of Lord Krishna at Brij as "impure", a move which, considering its sacredness to all Hindus, was a display of the most abject folly. The conflict was resolved by another battle, in which the Moghul forces were soundly defeated, but at the cost of a severe depletion of the strength of Mewar. Raj Singh was alone among Rajput rulers to dare to offer sanctuary to the defenders of Hindu shrines. Aurangzeb, somewhat chastened, concluded a treaty with Raj Singh's son, Maharana Jai Singh, in 1681; the terms were that certain lands of Mewar should be ceded to the Moghuls in return for exemption from that debilitating tax.

It was an honourable settlement, resulting in the complete withdrawal of the Moghul army from Mewar and a period of peace in Udaipur lasting some fifty years. This was the peace which enabled the painters of Mewar under Maharana Amar Singh II (1698–1710) to develop and perfect their art, becoming even more prolific under Maharana Sangram Singh II (1710–1734), when their work ventured on to a grander scale and provided a pictorial record of the ruler's life as well as of the customs and festivities of his people.

Incidentally, all subsequent Maharanas are descended from this Sangram, who had four sons, the first succeeding him on the *gadi* (Maharana Jagat Singh II), the other three each founding a new branch of the family—the Bagore line, the Karjali line, and the Shivrati line. The adoptions which became necessary when the senior line proved infertile in later generations were limited to the progeny of these three families.

Jagat Singh II (1734–1751), built the incredibly beautiful palace floating on the lake, which also bears his name—Jagniwas. Now known as the world-famous

Lake Palace, this elegant fantasy in white marble, covering an area of four acres shimmering on the waters, may claim to be among the most romantic creations of man. Intended as a retreat for the royal family during the stifling summer months, it is so constructed as to catch tiny breezes and waft them through columned courtyards, fountains and gardens, while the rooms themselves are delicately decorated with cusped arches, inlaid stones of pink and green lotus leaves, and painted mirrors. One room, the Khush Mahal, has seven windows entirely made of thick mosaic glass in a multitude of different coloured pieces, so fashioned to face the sun at dawn and throw across the cool floors of the room a dazzling display of splintered rainbow lights. No wonder this room is nowadays popular with honeymoon couples; it positively encourages a romantic disposition and invites a demonstration of affection.

Writing at the end of the last century, J. Fergusson was speechless with admiration for Jagniwas and Jagmandir. Only the Borromean Islands on Lake Maggiore could compare with them, he said, "but I need scarcely say their Indian rivals lose nothing by the comparison—they are as superior to them as the Duomo at Milan is to Buckingham Palace. Indeed, I know of nothing that will bear comparison with them anywhere."

Sangram was the last ruler to enjoy internal stability and freedom from outside interference. As Tod puts it, rather tendentiously, "Rana Sangram was the last prince who upheld the dignity of the *gadi* of Bappa Rawal. With his death commenced the Maratha ascendancy."

The Marathas, from a region south of the Rajput States, were a new and philistine enemy, devoid of all qualities save the pursuit of plunder, and with their arrival the Udaipur monarchy embarked upon a period of sad and sordid decay.

ARRIVAL OF THE BRITISH

The most painful truth about the Marathas was that they were Hindu. After hundreds of years of stolid refusal to be dominated first by Turks, then by Moghuls, that the one surviving Rajput state should now have to defend itself against Hindu brethren was too much to bear. Dispirited and bewildered, the people of Mewar more or less gave in. Or perhaps they simply did not believe it could happen.

Following the death of Emperor Aurangzeb in 1707, the Moghul court degenerated into squabbles for succession so destructive that it effectively collapsed as a coherent governing force within a very few years. The empire first disintegrated into separate self-governing states, then fell prey to Persian incursions from the north which, given their fragmented condition, they were powerless to withstand. Far more threatening, however, was the growth of the Marathas. In an effort to avoid eclipse, the remnants of the Moghul rulers made an alliance with the Marathas, according them the right to collect revenues. By the middle of the eighteenth century, the once-great Moghul Empire was at an end, and the Marathas were supreme. But they, too, suffered a collapse of central authority within a short time, and power passed to dozens of individual overlords on a local basis. Determined to attain their goals, unmindful of the havoc involved, they asserted themselves with great force, showing little interest in the culture or suffering of subjected races.

For the State of Mewar, it was a sorry sequel to centuries of proud and energetic defence. Having been alone among Rajputs in denying absolute authority to the Moghuls, alone in refusing to surrender their princesses in marriage to the invader, alone in maintaining their independence in scrupulous honour

Colonel James Tod

of their vow to Ekling ji, the Mewaris now found themselves engaged in perpetual warfare against a ruthless Hindu foe, and the vicious irony of their situation broke them. No power in India could stand against the Marathas, whose strength lay in their ignorance, their indifference, and minds impervious to suggestion or reflection. Their main tactic consisted in the rapid surprise movement of cavalry, and instant flight to safe harbour after attacking. They were less soldiers than looters, and in the face of their blunt aggression, Mewar suffered a series of dreadful defeats and humiliations.

The first Maratha invasion of Mewar took place in 1736. The next forty years, writes Tod, were "surcharged with evil. The Moghul princes observed at least the forms of government and justice, which occasionally tempered their aggressions; the Marathas were associations of vampires, who drained the very life-blood wherever the scent of spoil attracted them."

The man whose unhappy lot it was to preside over this tragedy was Maharana Jagat Singh II, who came to the throne in 1734, only two years before that first attack. He was therefore obliged to deal with disaster almost before he had time to arrange his ministry. Forced to entertain the Maratha leader, Baji Rao, at Udaipur that year, he began the annual payments of tribute to the invader which shortly were to destroy the country's economic base. Could the Maharana have been more energetic in his custody of his people's fate? Possibly. Tod, writing when the memory was still fresh in Mewar and the British were being welcomed, uncharacteristically, as saviours, offers an undilutedly critical assessment of his personality which may owe something to bias. "Addicted to pleasure, his habits of levity and profusion totally unfitted him for the task of governing his country at such a juncture", he says. "He considered his elephant fights of more importance than keeping down the Marathas. Like all his family he patronised the arts, greatly enlarged the palace, and expended £250,000 in embellishing the islands of the Pichola. The villas scattered over the valley were all erected by him, and many of those festivals devoted to idleness and dissipation, and now firmly rooted in Udaipur, were instituted by Jagat Singh II."

Art continued to flourish at court, and we now feel some gratitude to Jagat Singh for being the first Maharana to declare the names of individual artists in inscriptions; the miniaturists Jai Ram, Naga, Raghunath, and Bakhta were all active during his reign. Perhaps, by implication, this concern with the luxuries of life confirms Tod's damning indictment.

Whichever the case, there can scarcely be any mitigating excuses for the wilful idleness which typified the next four generations, some of whom bore illustrious names they did little to grace. Jagat Singh II was succeeded in 1751 by his son, Maharana Pratap Singh II, who reigned for three years and paid out vast sums to the Maratha overlords in return for a quiet life. As a consequence, his son Maharana Raj Singh II (1754–1761) was so poor that he had to borrow from a tribute-collector to pay for his own marriage. To make matters worse, he had a cruel and unattractive character. He was probably poisoned. Dying without heirs, he had adopted his uncle Ari to succeed him. Maharana Ari Singh II (1761–1773) is credited (if that be the word) with a vile temper which so alienated the court that his palace was a continual cauldron of intrigue and suspicion, the very faults which his ancestors had striven to avoid. Udaipur was actually under siege for six months during his reign, until the enemy was induced to withdraw upon receipt of a vast ransom. Capitulation of this kind was anathema to a true Rajput; the *sardar*s (nobleman) supported a pretender to the throne, Ratna, allegedly a posthumous son of Maharana Raj Singh, and a catastrophic civil war ensued. Ari Singh met his end, hardly unexpectedly, by assassination; he was murdered by a prince of Bundi while they were out hunting together, and it is assumed that his noblemen colluded in the act.

Ari Singh was succeeded in turn by two infant sons. Maharana Hamir Singh II (1773–1778) was totally ruled by his mother. The country then reached the nadir of its fortunes. Tod puts it thus: "The demoralisation of Mewar was complete; her fields were deluged with blood, and her soil was the prey of every paltry marauder."

Maharana Bhim Singh meeting with Sir Charles Metcalfe and James Tod, Mewar, c.1821
Attributed to artist Ghasi
Acc. No. 2010.T.0001

Maharana Bhim Singh succeeded his brother at the age of ten, the fourth minor to inherit the *gadi* in the space of forty years. Again, the influence of his mother as Queen Regent was so tenacious that she continued to rule in his stead long after he reached maturity. Tod, who knew him personally, said that he was "inefficient and averse to business. Vain shows, frivolous amusements and an irregular liberty alone occupied him. He had little steadiness of purpose and was particularly a prey to female influence [an obvious allusion to Mama]... his judgement was good, but he seldom followed its dictates; in short, he was adept in theory, and a novice in practice." Cleverly yet diplomatically, Tod contrived to make it clear that Bhim Singh was lazy, and left all decisions of state to others.

Bhim Singh was reduced to borrowing money from the ruler of Kota, who even paid the expenses of his wedding. He had numerous offspring (some say ninety-five sons, some say one hundred; anyway, a great many), but it is the tragic fate of his daughter, Krishna Kumari, which is chiefly remembered. The rulers of both Jaipur and Jodhpur wanted to marry her. Dependent as he was upon charity, and unwilling therefore to risk offending either monarch, Bhim Singh prevaricated; he would not declare in favour of one or the other, he did nothing at all. It was left to Krishna Kumari herself to resolve the dilemma. In the privacy of her quarters at the City Palace, she took poison and died. She was barely sixteen years old. Somewhat belatedly, Bhim Singh then made a decision; he turned one room in the City Palace into a shrine dedicated to the memory of her courage, and called it *Krishna Vilas*.

At the beginning of the nineteenth century, Udaipur was in all essentials under the control of a rapacious Maratha general called Ambaji, who amassed considerable personal wealth at the expense of the debilitated state. Gradually, its towns were abandoned and deserted by their starving inhabitants; the country, uncultivated, became a wilderness; and the Maharana himself was reduced to poverty. Such was the condition of the country when the British arrived in 1817, in the person of James Tod.

This is not the place to rehearse yet again the long and fascinating saga of British involvement in India. There are countless fine studies, some of which the reader will find in the bibliography at the end of this narrative. The shortest summary, paying particular attention to the affairs of Rajasthan, must suffice.

Britain had originally shown interest in India solely as a source of trade, the East India Company being established in the seventeenth century as a purely mercantile body devoted to the business of export for profit. Initially, there was no intention on the part of the British to build an empire in the East, nor did they feel any corresponding compunction about taking whatever they could find for their own purposes. The Dutch, the French, the Portuguese were all doing the same, and as the Moghul Empire dribbled to its unworthy close, the whole continent seemed ripe for investment. India became British by stealth, almost by accident, as the fortunes of the East India Company prospered and more and more British families made their homes in India. The trading company grew imperceptibly into an administrative class, then into a governing body, then into a quiet invader engaged in a conquest without arms.

As the tentacles of the East India Company spread ever farther afield, control of their extremities became impossible to oversee. Individual officers of the Company, unelected and unrepresentative, but intoxicated with the kind of haughty power which appeared theirs for the asking and was quite forbidden them in their own country, grew as greedy as the Marathas. There were instances of collaboration with the marauders for the soulless exploitation of local inhabitants.

The British Government, which took over management of the East India Company in 1772, appointing Warren Hastings its first Governor-General, was genuinely appalled when it discovered the inequities which were taking place in its name. Envoys were sent to the Princely States, of which there were then five hundred and sixty-two, in an attempt to restore order and curtail the personal acquisitiveness of the Government's servants. The man sent to Udaipur was James Tod. What he found was a State which had reverted in

Treaty between the Honourable The English East India Company and Maharana Bheem Sing Rana of Oudeipoor, concluded by Mr Charles Theophilus Metcalfe, on the part of The Honourable Company, in virtue of full powers granted by His Excellency The Most Noble The Marquess of Hastings K.G. Governor General, and by Thakoor Ajeet Sing, on the part of the Maharana, in virtue of full powers conferred by the Maharana aforesaid—

First Article

There shall be perpetual Friendship Alliance and Unity of Interests between the two States from Generation to Generation, and the Friends and Enemies of one shall be the Friends and Enemies of both—

Second Article

The British Government engages to protect the Principality and Territory of Oudeipoor—

Third Article

The Maharana of Oudeipoor will always act in subordinate cooperation with the British Government, and acknowledge its supremacy; and will not have any connexion with other Chiefs or States—

Fourth

The Treaty of 1818

its political administration to the feudal conditions which had applied in the twelfth century, with a weak ruler and disaffected noblemen, some reduced to the condition of beggars by the predators.

He returned in 1818 not as the representative of a trading company but as one of the newly-appointed Political Agents, assigned to Udaipur, bearing a treaty in his hands. Maharana Bhim Singh welcomed both him and the treaty with undisguised relief.

British influence, which by 1818 had covered the whole sub-continent, stopped the Marathas dead in their tracks and put an end to what threatened to be a complete takeover. The British presence had secured other advantages for India apart from the imposition of peace. Lord Wellesley's wholesale annexation of territory had made possible the application of a coherent policy, bringing the multitude of disparate elements in India beneath the umbrella of one legislative authority.

Lord Macaulay had single-handedly drawn up a new penal code which would apply to the whole sub-continent and which remains, even today, the basis of Indian law. This was another step towards the principle of equality before the law, and it is ironic that Macaulay, remembered in England for his authorship of one of the best historical works ever written, in India should be chiefly renowned as a legislator.

Then, the foundation of the Asiatic Society encouraged the study of Indian culture, even at the expense of European literature. Though there had been many British bone-heads unresponsive to the richness of the various cultures which surrounded them, and who had suggested that nothing would benefit the Indians so much as a good English library, the adherents of the Asiatic Society approached their land of adoption with some humility and respect. Colonel Steward of the Society averred that Hinduism was in no need of Christian correction. Hindu mythology, he wrote, was "the most complete and ample system of Moral Allegory that the world has ever produced."

ANNALS AND ANTIQUITIES

OF

RAJAST'HAN,

OR THE

CENTRAL AND WESTERN RAJPOOT STATES

OF

INDIA.

BY

LIEUTENANT-COLONEL JAMES TOD,

Late Political Agent to the Western Rajpoot States.

VOL. I.

London:

PUBLISHED BY SMITH, ELDER, AND Co., 65, CORNHILL;

AND

CALKIN AND BUDD, Booksellers to his Majesty, PALL-MALL.

1829.

Title page of Tod's *Annals and Antiquities of Rajasthan*, 1829

Finally, there was that curious unspoken alliance between the British and the Indians on a personal level, which had been quite unlike anything that had occurred under the conquerors of earlier times, and would one day be recognised as a mysterious and unique example of bonding between occupied territories and the occupying power. Of course, it did not happen overnight, but took years to evolve; nevertheless, its growth and importance cannot really be denied. More than anyone else, Queen Victoria exemplified its charm. She never went to India, yet she experienced a strangely intense feeling for the people, as is amply demonstrated by her diaries. She made valiant attempts to learn Hindi and Urdu. In return, the Indians revered her like one of their own native gods. Geoffrey Moorhouse wrote, "There can scarcely in all history have been an absentee monarch who touched as many different subjects as Queen Victoria did with a sense of mystery approaching the divine... her own personality was considered exempt from the natural resentments of a conquered people." When the time came for her to assume her role as empress, she insisted that complete religious toleration be written into the Proclamation, otherwise she would not sign it. Victoria usually got her way.

Those tenacious hierarchies which underlay Indian society as much as British also helped to form the cement between the two peoples. The British, imprisoned by their own class system, appreciated the purpose of Hindu caste even if they could not hope to plumb its subtleties. In their understanding of the natural function of hierarchical structures, the Indian and the British were brothers.

The treaties which the British invited the Princely States to sign were more or less identical. Udaipur was guaranteed protection from any future invasion, and help in the restoration of all its hereditary territories. The Maharana's sovereignty within his own country would be respected, subject to co-operation with a Political Agent in recognition of "perpetual alliance and friendship" with the East India Company. The Agent would not interfere with the affairs of Udaipur unless gross mismanagement should occur. In return, Maharana Bhim Singh agreed to abstain from political correspondence with the rulers of other States, to submit disputes to the arbitration of the British government, and to surrender one quarter of the state's revenue as tribute for five years, the contribution to be increased to three-eighths thereafter in perpetuity.

The treaty was signed on 13 January, 1818. Colonel Tod, as Political Agent, quickly discerned that Udaipur had fallen into such apathy and anarchy that his role would need to be more than advisory, and he set about reorganising the State's economy. Within two years he had doubled the revenue. In a very real sense, for a time Colonel Tod was *de facto* ruler of Udaipur.

The State was indeed fortunate in having Tod to take charge of its affairs, for not only was he a capable administrator, but far more importantly, he was a sensitive and widely educated man, cultured in the best sense of the term, that is, ever willing to learn as well as to teach. Overwhelmed by the beauty and majesty of Mewar's past, he was moved by an admiration for Rajput qualities so profound that he determined they should be known and appreciated by the world outside. His book, *The Annals and Antiquities of Rajasthan*, is the glorious result. It is no exaggeration to say that Tod's involvement with Rajasthan was a love story, and his *Annals* the declaration of that love. Quite apart from its being a massive enterprise of original research, and a masterpiece of Gibbonian prose, it is touched with emotion on nearly every page. In his own way, Tod deserves a place among the heroes of Mewar, along with Kumbha, Sanga, Pratap and Fateh Singh. His memory is justly held in affection.

Tod's own remarks on the mutual advantages of Britain's protection of Udaipur merit quotation. "As long as we respect their established usages", he wrote, "and by contributing to the prosperity of the people preserve our motives from distrust, it will be a barrier impenetrable to invasion." With these words did Tod quietly subscribe his own signature to the ancient traditions of service inaugurated by the vow of Bappa Rawal and, without presumption, permit himself to be an honorary disciple of Ekling ji.

The Mor Chowk (the peacock courtyard) in the City Palace Museum

VICTORIAN STABILITY

It would be foolish to pretend that Colonel Tod's undertaking to reform Udaipur's finances was lightly made. Under Bhim Singh the state had begun seriously to fall into arrears in its payment of tribute to the British, and when he died in 1828 ("having learnt neither humility from affliction nor wisdom from poverty, he held fast by his faults and weakness to his death"), the debt had accumulated alarmingly. Matters grew worse under his son, Maharana Jawan Singh (1828–1838) who, with the departure of Colonel Tod and the removal of his restraining influence, gave himself over to debauchery, vice and unbridled extravagance. He drank, paid little attention to affairs of state, and assumed the British would look after everything, leaving him to enjoy himself. The British government had eventually to warn him that if debts were not liquidated, some territorial security would be demanded.

Mewar painting continued to flourish both under Bhim Singh, whose foremost court artist was Chokha, and Jawan Singh, who moved away from Rajput tradition to imitate Western-style portraiture. The artist Tara Chand was himself painted by William Carpenter, and this fine portrait, revelatory of much compassion and intelligence, may now be seen at the Victoria and Albert Museum in London.

From Jawan Singh's time comes a story for which no documentary evidence has been found but which, on the principle that rumours do not generate themselves, is repeated here for what it is worth. The palace often called upon *nautch* girls for a variety of purposes. They were used to initiate young princes in the mysteries of carnal love, and to entertain with dancing and acrobatics. One such was promised half the kingdom if she could walk on a tightrope stretched across the lake from the City Palace. It was all a splendid jest and nobody expected her to succeed. Knowing full well that *nautch* girls were expendable, the Maharana and his noblemen assembled to watch the feat in a spirit of levity. To their consternation, however, the girl showed every sign of reaching her destination and invoking the famed Rajput code of honour, whereupon one of the men severed the rope with his sword and she plunged into the lake. Before she perished, she found breath to cast a curse upon the family, swearing that no Maharana would thenceforth be blessed with a direct heir. Given the character of Jawan Singh, it is not altogether unlikely that he could have been a party to such a wager when in the throes of one of his bouts of intoxication. It is a fact that, of the seven Maharanas who ascended the *gadi* in the course of the next hundred or so years, six had to be adopted.

The first of these was Jawan Singh's successor. Having no issue of his own, he adopted a cousin from the Bagore branch of the family, who was invested as Maharana Sardar Singh in 1848. His short rule of four years was undistinguished, being marked by quarrels at court and a further increase of debts to the British. He adopted the younger of his two brothers, Swarup, to succeed him.

With the rule of Maharana Swarup Singh, 70th of the line, some of the dignity of Udaipur was restored. He was the first ruler since the Treaty of 1818 to pay serious attention to state affairs and make his priority the payment of arrears in tribute. This he achieved simply by reducing extravagance at court. On the other hand, his deeply conservative nature brought him frequently into conflict with the British, he anxious to uphold Rajput tradition while they insisted he modernise and embrace values more in line with their conception of what was civilised. A particular difference of approach erupted over the practice of *sati*—the "voluntary" self-cremation of widows immediately after the death of an honoured husband. As recently as 1838, three wives and six concubines had committed *sati* on the death of Maharana Jawan Singh.

The British instructed Swarup Singh to ban *sati*. He resisted, claiming it was a religious rite which outsiders should not interfere with. They said nonsense, it was no more than compulsory suicide, and therefore an outrage. Of course, to a Christian, suicide was a sin so heinous it forfeited God's power to forgive. To a Rajput it was nothing of the kind; on the contrary, it was considered dishonourable ("sinful" if you like) for a dead chief to be burnt alone. Swarup Singh thought that the very essence of his inheritance would be at stake were he to be forced to do something regarded by his forefathers as wholly wrong. But forced he was, and *sati* was legally banned in Udaipur.

Part of the trouble lay in the personality of the Political Agent, Major Robinson, who, unlike his predecessor-but-one Tod, was arrogant and insensitive. He could not accustom himself to the injustice (as he saw it) of an obstinately feudal system which kept the masses in poverty and illiteracy while law remained solely the prerogative of the Maharana's will. Conversely, Swarup Singh could never get used to rule by legislation, which he saw as an infringement of his personal duty. And so the British boldly clipped his wings and made his authority largely symbolic. No longer free to rule as he wished, the Maharana became resentful of his dependence and sank into a sullen life of sensual self-indulgence.

Everything changed with the arrival of a new Political Agent and the upheaval which has become known to history as the Indian Mutiny of 1857. It would be a mistake to think of this insurgency as the first strike in a struggle for national independence. It was not. It was an explosion of frustration at the apparent indifference of the British to deeply-entrenched customs, frustration which in future generations would deepen and evolve into the basis for a national identity. The changes which the British attempted to introduce (and no doubt expected to be thanked for) were profoundly shocking to most Indians. The introduction of the English language and culture, the imposition of railway trains (a gross and devilish machine insulting to Hindu peace), the desire to abolish caste, all were pursued with scant regard for local sensibilities. Intended to wrest India from the stranglehold of its mediaeval grip, these measures instead brought offence and bewilderment.

The immediate cause of the Mutiny was a typical instance of this rift in understanding. A new grease for lubricating rifles came into use; Hindus would not touch beef fat and Muslims would not touch pork fat (they were meant to bite the head off the cartridge, which would bring fat into contact with the lips). The British military, devoid of that intelligence which informed the best echelons of the Civil Service, and overtly condescending towards "natives", insisted that they should do as they were told. Rebellion ensued, and both the atrocities committed and the scale of British vengeance were terrifying.

The point of the story for Udaipur is interesting. The new Political Agent, Lieutenant-Colonel Lawrence, was conciliatory and diplomatic, alert to the Maharana's beliefs and careful not to belittle them. He persuaded Swarup Singh to be helpful to the British, who were running in fear of the catastrophe they had unleashed, and there followed an extraordinary example of compassion which would astonish anyone who had watched the course of Swarup Singh's past conflicts with the occupying power, had they but known the family's legacy of honourable conduct towards a foe.

The Maharana gave sanctuary to frightened British refugees, women and children, harbouring them on the island of Jagmandir and personally guaranteeing their safety. (Jagmandir had been the refuge of the Moghul Prince Khurram—Shah Jahan—two centuries earlier.) He visited them in person more than once, and according to one witness, "nothing could exceed his civility and kindness." More than this, he urged others to behave in like manner, giving as his opinion that India should be grateful to the British for restoring order. Following his lead, villagers in the surrounding countryside also protected refugees and refused to surrender them to the less scrupulous demands of extremists. "You have eaten with us and are our guests", they said, "and now if you were our greatest enemy we would defend you."

So moved was she by this display of clemency that Queen Victoria thanked the Maharana for his support. He in turn wrote to the Queen a personal letter to congratulate her on successfully quelling the mutineers. Udaipur had come a

To His Highness The Maharana of

Oodeypore.

Highness,

      I have received the commands of my Sovereign, Queen Victoria, to convey to Your Highness the thanks of Her Majesty for your very friendly letter, transmitted through His Excellency, the Governor General of India.

      During the recent disastrous period of the military insurrection in Upper India, The Queen relied with confidence on the unshaken fidelity, with which Your Highness and the other friendly representatives of the ancient houses of Rajpootana had adhered to your engagements with the British Government, and Her Majesty observed, with the liveliest gratification, the support which you gave to her Armies, the assistance which you rendered to her subjects, and the tranquillity which you maintained throughout your extensive dominions. It is in such times that the quality of friendship is best seen, and Her Majesty commands me to assure you that the proofs which Your Highness has afforded of loyalty and devotion to the British Crown will ever be held by Her Majesty in grateful remembrance.

      That Your Highness may enjoy length of days and continued prosperity, is the earnest prayer of

           Your Highness' friend
           and well-wisher,

           Charles Wood

India Office,
  London.
November 30th, 1859.

The Mutiny Letter

long way since the disagreements which had disfigured the early part of Swarup Singh's reign.

The immediate upshot of the Indian Mutiny was the final disbandment of the East India Company and its replacement by direct Crown rule. Henceforth, India would be part of the British Empire. Queen Victoria's Royal Proclamation of 1858 contained the famous sentence, "We shall respect the rights, honour and dignity of the Native Princes as Our own." Subtly, with hardly anyone noticing, the Rajput kings were thus demoted to "princes", and given the consolation prize of a new title, "Highness", which they had never used before. Their emasculation under what Virginia Fass has called the "stultifying security" of British rule had begun.

An attempt was made to persuade the Maharana into journeying to England to be received by Victoria. In the Royal Archives at Windsor a letter from the Bombay Commander-in-Chief waxes lyrically about the azure waters of Lake Pichola "margined by sharp hills and studded with emerald islands, fertile in orange groves (and lodges) and innocent of agrarian outrages", and goes on to describe Swarup Singh's status in breathless tones:

> As the apex of Hindu dynasties, on one day of the year His Highness, who is his own Archbishop, receives divine worship, but is, as a corrective to presumptuous sin, on other occasions required to send round to his kindred nobles, the Insignia of Sovereignty. He is believed to be descended from the Sun and Moon, and on the festival of the latter, must clothe himself, his Wives, his attendants and his furniture in a Livery of silver tissue. Could he be induced to follow the example of the Nizam [of Hyderabad] and visit England, to do homage to his Empress, such precedent, it is said, would break down the prejudices, which by the rules of Hindu caste, attach to crossing "the Black Water".

Maharana Swarup Singh was not to be so undermined or purchased. He did not go to London. Even in death, he struck a blow for the independence of his ways which infuriated the British. An act of forbidden *sati* took place despite the fact that all his wives declined the honour. A slave-girl was persuaded that great credit would rebound upon her if she would consent to take their place. As Swarup's favourite concubine, she was even eager for the privilege. Colonel Eden, who witnessed the event, relates what happened:

> The royal corpse, dressed up in regal attire, was conveyed from the palace to the burning-place (called the Maha Sati) in a species of sedan-chair; the funeral procession, composed of all loyal subjects of the State, one and all, high and low, rich and poor, even the successor to the throne, proceeded the whole distance on foot; one alone in this vast multitude was allowed to ride, and she had but a short time to live. Mounted on a gorgeously caparisoned horse; herself richly attired as for a festive occasion, literally covered with jewels and costly ornaments; her hair loose and in disorder; her whole countenance wild with the excitement of the scene and the intoxicating effect of the drugs she had swallowed, she issued forth with the body. As customary on such occasions, the victim, as the procession moved on, unclasped the ornaments with which she was profusely decorated, and flung them to the right and to the left amongst the crowd. On reaching the Maha Sati, in a space closed by tent walls, the corpse was unrobed, and the slave girl seating herself with the head of the lifeless body in her lap was built up, as it were, with wood steeped in oil. The kanats or canvas wails were then removed, and the pyre lighted; and as the flame shot up bright and fierce, the crowd around raised a great clamour, which lasted until the dreadful scene was over.

One month before he died, Swarup Singh adopted a fourteen-year-old boy from his own branch of the family, in fact his great-nephew, to succeed him. The boy, Shambhu Singh, was placed on the *gadi* of Udaipur in 1861, even as the funeral of his great-uncle was taking place; this was normal procedure to avoid any interregnum.

One year later, the British Government (whose right to meddle in matters of succession was reluctantly accepted for the sake of order) accorded to Maharana Shambhu Singh the right to adopt his own heir; this he eventually did. But for the moment his attentions were drawn in a different direction. It was probably not entirely his fault, for his vulnerable youth was exploited by flatterers, but Shambhu Singh's early reign was notable for a degree of personal and sexual license which shocked the Victorian prudes in the Political Agent's office. His private life was said to be "disgraceful", and it was observed that he was "encouraged to be lewd", presumably by favourites—older people, who should have known better. Whoever they were, these people gained such influence over the young Maharana that he banished all courtiers who disapproved of his way of life, including his mother and uncle, who attempted to restrain him.

The administration of the State was fortunately safe. While Shambhu Singh was still a minor, his official duties were taken over by a council, with the advice and assistance of the Political Agent, Lt-Col. Eden, who thereby came to exercise considerable powers in the governance of Udaipur. At his instigation, many reforms were introduced. Important roads were laid, much-needed repairs were made to public utilities, the police force was reorganised and given a new sense of purpose, so that life and property were to be better protected; also, the civil and criminal courts were improved. All this was the work of Lt-Col. Eden, and consequently the cause of some resentment among the people (who still respectfully considered the British to be interlopers), but so well did he manage the administration that when the British government handed over control to Shambhu Singh in 1865, investing him with the full powers of his State, the treasury coffers showed a very heavy credit balance. The Maharana was then eighteen.

His licentiousness consigned to the past, Shambhu Singh continued the reforms already begun in his name, and added considerably to them. In particular, he tackled the dreadful conditions of the famine of 1869 with maturity and compassion. He was illiterate, but appreciated the value of education and built several schools. He went so far as to learn English himself, possibly the first of his family ever to do so. Shambhu Singh was an odd mixture of contradictions, for despite his encouragement of education, he was personally a slave to superstition, and despite his firm adherence to Hindu spirituality, his court was in many ways materialistic, a fertile source of intrigue and rumour.

It was Shambhu Singh who built an entirely new palace next to the main one, and which is now absorbed into the City Palace Complex. This is Shambhu Niwas Palace, the tall, elegant, turreted and domed mansion which used, before the latter was built, to perch dominantly at the very edge of a steep hill. Its lower storeys are now hidden by the wall of Shiv Niwas Palace, but it is still in use, and is currently the residence of Shriji Arvind Singh Mewar.

Shambhu was decorated by Queen Victoria in 1871, and died at the early age of twenty-seven in 1874. His death was marked by uproar in the palace on two accounts: first, the women tried to kill themselves, and second, the succession was hotly contested.

It appears that the British, in the guise of the then Political Agent, Colonel Wright, had to intervene to stop *sati* occurring. The Viceroy wrote saying that he "commends Colonel Wright for his firm conduct on the death of the Maharana of Udaipur when he prevented the women in the *zenana* from destroying themselves and preserved the peace till the new ruler was established." The Secretary for India in Disraeli's government, Lord Salisbury, also wrote to inform Queen Victoria:

> Lord Salisbury with his humble duty to Your Majesty respectfully submits an account of the death of the Maharana of Udaipur and the nomination of his successor. The papers are of interest as detailing the mode in which the ceremony of sati was for the first time prevented in that State on the occasion of the death of a reigning Prince.

The turmoil surrounding the succession was even more problematic. It was suspected Shambhu Singh might have been poisoned by his uncles, but British doctors who investigated could find no trace of poison in his body. They concluded that his mysterious illness might be the result of the excesses of his adolescence. The succession had already been secured by having the Maharana adopt his first cousin, Sajjan Singh, as his son. Sajjan Singh was yet another minor. When he came to the *gadi* with such dramatic suddenness, he was still only sixteen years old.

But the habits of conspiracy lingered. Sajjan's right to the throne was disputed by his uncle Sohan Singh. Lord Salisbury refers to this in his letter to Queen Victoria:

> The Queen Mother [i.e. Shambhu's mother] vehemently opposed this nomination [of Sajjan] and a curious account of the intrigues which took place appears wherein poisonings, witchcraft and other devices are spoken of. A curious telegram is printed at the commencement of the papers from Sohan Singh—the claimant—asking the Government not to recognize Sajjan Singh and enclosing six shillings for the answer.

> The installation of the young Maharana was delayed because the Brahmins on casting the horoscope found the present moment impropitious. Colonel Wright, suspecting they had been bribed by Sohan Singh, directed that the Brahmins must at once be told to read the horoscope differently. Accordingly, they ascertained that the influence of an evil star had been counteracted by a lucky one and the ceremonies then took place at once, ending with an elephant fight.

Unwilling to heed repeated warnings, Sohan Singh declined to give his allegiance to the new Maharana, was arrested, and imprisoned at Benares for six years. He was permitted to return to Udaipur in 1880 on condition he submit to certain restrictions on his freedom.

As it happened, the failure of Sohan Singh's revolt was extremely fortunate for Udaipur, for after Sajjan Singh was invested with full powers at the age of eighteen, he continued and even accelerated the reforms inaugurated by his predecessor. He was a very modern, forward-looking man who perceived the need to bring his State in line with contemporary conditions and so increase its prosperity. Among the many achievements of his reign were the establishment of a High Court wherein, for the first time, the Judiciary was made entirely independent of the Executive; the formation of new government departments to deal with accounts, forestry, and public works; and the setting up of an Education Committee and a History Department. (On forestry, Sajjan Singh was a hundred years ahead of his time, making plans to arrest the silting up of Lake Pichola caused by progressive deforestation of the surrounding hills.)

Under this Maharana, Udaipur was the second town in India after Bombay to form a municipality, and one of the first among Rajput states to establish a government press charged with the regular publication of a Gazette to keep the people informed of policies and programmes pursued by their Administration. In short, by a gigantic personal effort, he forced Udaipur to become efficient and streamlined.

More than that, Sajjan Singh emulated the style of his illustrious ancestor, Rana Kumbha, in his devotion to study and the arts. Though not well educated to begin with, he was eager for self-improvement and soon developed a taste for literature and philosophy, in which disciplines he grew so adept that he wrote poetry himself, remarkable for its reflection and allusiveness. Sajjan Singh patronised and honoured scholarship, daily conversing with learned men at his court on abstruse metaphysical concepts. His most famous scholar was Kaviraja Shyamaldas, author of the *Veer Vinod*, an exhaustive history of the kingdom of Mewar written in Hindi and still a major source for historians. Kaviraja was appointed curator of the Sajjan Vani Vilas Library established by this progressive and thoughtful Maharana, whose comparative youth made him all the more energetic in the pursuit of knowledge.

Building work also continued apace. The large public garden, known as Sajjan Niwas, was laid out at this time, affording the people of Udaipur their first opportunity for a restful stroll amid the shade of trees, far from the din of city life. (He acquired several other gardens and incorporated them within it, adding a zoo.) Sajjangarh, high on the hill overlooking Lake Pichola on the opposite side from the City Palace, was erected, but never properly used, as it proved impossible to pump water up to it. Numerous reparations and maintenance work were carried out at Chittor, including the rebuilding of Padmini's water pavilion. Finally, some important irrigation construction took place, of lasting benefit to the community.

In recognition of Sajjan Singh's signal accomplishments, Queen Victoria awarded him the Star of India in 1881, an honour he was at first disposed to decline as being beneath him. He reasoned that the senior representative of descendants of the Sun (Suryavanshis) should not be demeaned by the decoration of a mere star! By this reckoning, he and his line of Maharanas had more right to the appellation "Sun King" than had Louis XIV of France, accorded this doubtful distinction by European historians. Nevertheless, he relented and accepted the decoration in due course, as a token of respect from one monarch to another. To mark the occasion, he entertained Lord Ripon in lavish manner at Chittor, and wrote a charming letter to him which is still at Windsor:

> I wish sincerely to express the great pleasure I have experienced in meeting Your Excellency today along with my Sirdars in this time-honoured city of Chittor, which is considered by one and all of us so famous and so very dear, for the defence and possession of which so many of my ancestors have in years gone by sacrificed their precious lives. In commemoration of this the Sisodia chieftains of Mewar have all ever since borne the title of Chitoda.

> Our meeting today is the outflow of mutual feelings of regard which have existed between the British Government and the Mewar State ever since the year 1818, and in proof that this kindly feeling still exists Your Excellency has invested me on behalf of Her Majesty the Queen-Empress of India with the Honourable Insignia of the Star of India of which most exalted order Her Majesty has been

graciously pleased to appoint me a Knight Grand Commander, a title which will tend to increase and make more enduring our mutual bond of union.

I receive this honour with the greatest pleasure and beg most heartily to thank Her Imperial Majesty and Your Excellency, being fully confident that this distinction will conduce to the welfare and prosperity of my State and people ... May Her Majesty the Queen-Empress have a long, happy and prosperous reign, and may Your Excellency's management of Indian State affairs be as beneficial to the people as creditable to yourself, and thereby leave in the hearts and minds of the people of India a lasting memorial of Your Excellency's Viceroyalty.

Maharana Sajjan Singh revived the glory and pride of his race with an abundant display of enthusiasm in a very short time. The approbation and happiness of his people were more important to him than any foreign recognition, as a careful reading of this letter will confirm, and his name was long revered by grateful subjects. Sadly, his life was cut short. He died at the desperately early age of twenty-six, even younger than his predecessor. Posterity will never know what he might have achieved had he lived a normal span.

Maharana Fateh Singh (1884–1930) in *durbar* with the Resident and other English guests

Photograph by Johnston & Hoffmann, 1880–1900
Acc. No. 2008.06.0278

BACK TO FATEH SINGH

Sajjan Singh, once more, died without an heir. His wife had given birth to a son two years before, in 1882, but the child did not survive. Another adoption was clearly necessary. This time, there was a general consensus that the choice should not again fall upon an adolescent, but on a man of mature years. The family and noblemen unanimously selected Fateh Singh, aged thirty-five and already married, the third son in the Shivrati family, cousins of the Udaipur line. Fateh Singh was thus descended from the fourth son of Maharana Sangram Singh II (1710–1734), from whose offspring, as we pointed out earlier, all adoptions had perforce to come.

Fateh Singh was chosen largely because his simple, rustic, pious life marked him out as a suitably pliant and docile man whose actions could be bent to the demands of the noblemen. Or so they thought. He turned out to be a huge surprise, the massively charismatic and impressive ruler with whom we started this narrative. Far from being malleable, one of his first actions on ascending the *gadi* in 1885 was to discipline the *sardar*s, who assumed they would be able to take advantage of his ignorance and inexperience to satisfy their own blatant appetite for power. He restored them to the dignified but subordinate position they should traditionally occupy. They were palpably shocked.

The long reign of Maharana Fateh Singh completely overturned the secondary role which British paramountcy had insidiously imposed upon Rajput rulers. Throughout the nineteenth century some rulers had tended to rely upon the British to ensure their survival, even if only as rather gorgeous fossils, and this reliance had perhaps rendered them "soft". They had surrendered their proud warrior status in return for prestige meted out to them by the British monarch.

They were granted a certain number of gun salutes in accordance with their "rank" (in ascending scale up to twenty-one, Udaipur being deemed worthy of nineteen); spurious coats of arms were invented for them; honours and favours were lavished upon them; some were made ADCs to Queen Victoria, others were permitted to entertain British envoys in lavish regal style. In such ways were they mollified, flattered, maintained in opulent indolence and impotence like splendidly caparisoned courtesans to be gazed upon. As Kipling wrote, "Providence created the Maharajahs to offer mankind a spectacle", and at that time it was no doubt a just observation. The consequence of all these trappings threatened to be disastrous to the unique bond of *raja* and *praja*, that relationship of trust which obtained between ruler and people. Hinduism placed significant importance on humility and simplicity, and these values were in danger of being smothered by luxurious ostentation. Moreover, the people could see that they were.

Even the orgy of building which took place in the nineteenth century, rivalling that of the Moghul period three centuries before, subtly altered from being a celebration of the glory of heritage to being an exercise is self-aggrandizement. "It was ironic", wrote Virginia Fass, "that the princes were only able to build monuments to their own royal grandeur when they themselves were subordinate to another imperial power."

The British were undeniably clever and cunning. They exalted the princes, but stopped short of allowing them to consider themselves true kings. Any attempt to refer to the *gadi* as a "throne" was roundly condemned; to call it a *gadi* was to underline, in British eyes, its status as a pretence in a kind of antique game—a mere folly.

They did not anticipate the arrival of Fateh Singh. Udaipur had nearly always managed to stand aloof from the beguiling temptations of British flattery, but no one was more disdainful of their approaches than the new Maharana with the cleft beard. From the beginning, he made it perfectly clear that he was not Maharana by grace of any Queen of England, but by order of his own people and in the service of Ekling ji. For half a century, he never wavered from this sacred conviction, and the British were obliged, for the most part, to acquiesce.

They tried, of course, to cajole him and buy his gratitude. On the occasion of Queen Victoria's Diamond Jubilee in 1897 they raised Udaipur's salute to twenty-one guns, the maximum. Along with Jaipur and Jodhpur, the Political Agent had already been upgraded to British Resident, with his own sumptuous mansion in town, as a mark of the special importance attached to Udaipur in the British Empire. None of this had the slightest effect on Fateh Singh, who continued to be sublimely indifferent to whatever ploys the British might invent; that was their own affair, not his.

Which is not to say he was impolite. To mark the Queen's Jubilee, he built Victoria Hall in Sajjan Niwas Garden. But its use was strictly for the people of Udaipur, as Fateh housed within it the library established by Maharana Sajjan Singh and made it public.

We shall not need to repeat the many facets of Fateh Singh's admirable character, related in some detail in Chapter One. His honesty, his exquisite manners, the awesome effect of his presence, all made it abundantly clear that he was statesman and sovereign par excellence. There was no question but that he was regarded as the most noble and most august monarch in India, the guardian and symbol of Hindu pride.

Two occasions on which he caused umbrage in British hearts have passed into Indian folklore. These were the famous *durbar*s held in Delhi in 1903 and 1911. (A *durbar* is an assembly of king and courtiers, a kind of ceremonial audience. It was adopted by Rajput kings from Moghul custom, and kidnapped by the British as an excuse for imperial pomp; they certainly had no practical use for it.) Fateh Singh went to the Delhi *durbar* of 1903 in two trains, accompanied by one thousand servants and retainers. He had been assured by Lord Curzon that he would enjoy pride of place in deference to the pre-eminence of Mewar, and that he would not be required to make obeisance. When he discovered that his position in the procession was to be *after* Hyderabad, Mysore, Kashmir and Baroda, in stark contrast to the promise made, he declined to make complaint. He simply refused to get out of his train, turned straight back, and left Delhi while the *durbar* was still in progress. The snub was pointed and effective. Loud were the protestations at the Maharana's effrontery, and much appalled astonishment was expressed. It was, however, no part of his purpose to be rude—on the contrary, he was the most sensitive and courteous of men. But he would not countenance any dilution of his revered role; it was a question of duty.

Similarly, he defied instructions to be present at the famous *durbar* in 1911, the most grandiose spectacle ever to take place in Indian history, which King George V himself attended. Word was spread in advance that the Maharana might not appear, causing consternation at the Residency. A former Resident, Claude Hill, wrote a letter which shows how Fateh commanded such respect that he had to be handled with kid gloves:

> My dear Friend,
>
> I have heard a rumour that there is some difficulty in connection with Your Highness' visit to Delhi and the seating in Durbar. As Your Highness' most sincere friend, do permit me to beg of you not to allow anything to interfere with your willing attendance. I know that Your Highness may feel that the position accorded is not that to which you are strictly, in Your Highness' view, entitled; but I would ask Your Highness to take the wider view of your responsibility on this unique occasion. Any occurrence which should mar the harmony of the visit of the King Emperor to Delhi would be deplorable; but it would be doubly so, if the occurrence were occasioned by the attitude of the head of the Sisodia Rajputs, whose loyalty is so far truer than is the case with some others. Think what would be said by Your Highness' enemies! How Your Highness would be misrepresented by them! Is it not worthwhile to sacrifice something rather than to appear in the eyes of India as the cause of a break in the harmony with which all

classes hope to welcome His Imperial Majesty? I hope, indeed, that the rumour I have heard is incorrect, and that there is no question of trouble; but my affectionate regard for Your Highness is such that I have felt compelled to write out of my heart what I feel; and I know that Your Highness will appreciate the motives which activate me in writing. Believe me,

Your Highness' very sincere friend,
Claude Hill

Fateh's reply has not survived. At least Hill understood him, which is more than can be said for the current Resident, who wrote to inform him that "His Imperial Majesty the King Emperor has been pleased to appoint Your Highness to be ruling Chief-in-Waiting during His Imperial Majesty's stay in Delhi." Such a titbit was unlikely to tempt him.

One story has it that Fateh Singh threatened to commit suicide rather than allow the dignity of the House of Mewar to be impaired, but this does not accord well with his gentle nature. After long and patient persuasion, he did after all make the journey to Delhi, but still did not attend the *durbar*. His chair, made for the occasion, was never sat upon. What then happened was unique. George V came to Delhi railway station to meet him, thus making Fateh the first Indian ruler to meet the King Emperor in private audience. After congratulating the King as one sovereign to another, the Maharana returned to Udaipur, allowing the magnificent *durbar* to proceed without him.

Other rulers were meantime joyfully competing with each other in the splendour of their garments and the ornamentation of their elephants.

The Maharana was criticised for his refusal to raise a battalion of troops to fight for the British during the Great War of 1914–1918, offering merely to provide 200 camels, which the British accurately recognised as a derisory snub. However, his reasoning was persuasive. He is reported to have remarked, "When there is a fight in India, Europeans do not come here to die, so why should we

THE RESIDENCY,
RAJKOT.

27ᵗʰ Nov:

My dear Friend

I have heard a rumour that there is some difficulty in connection with Your Highness' visit to Delhi and seating in Durbar.

As Your Highness most sincere friend, do permit me to beg of you not to allow anything to interfere with your willing attendance. I know that Your Highness may feel that the position accorded is

Sisodia Rajputs, whose loyalty so far truer than is the case with some others. Think what would be said by Your Highness' Enemies! How Your Highness would be misrepresented by them!

Is it not worth while to sacrifice something rather than to appear in the eyes of India as the cause of a break in the harmony with which all classes hope to welcome His Imperial Majesty?

not that to which you are strictly, in Your Highness view, entitled; but I would ask Your Highness to take the wider view of your responsibility on this unique occasion. Any occurrence which should mar the harmony of the visit of the King Emperor to Delhi would be deplorable; & it would be doubly so, if the occurrence were occasioned by the attitude of the head of the

I hope, indeed, that the rumour I have heard is incorrect, & that there is no question of trouble: but my affectionate regard for Your Highness is such that I have felt compelled to write out of my heart what I feel; and I know that Your Highness will appreciate the motives which actuate me in writing. Believe me,

Your Highness' very sincere friend

Claude H Hill

Letter from Claude Hill to Maharana Fateh Singh

send out Indians to die when Europeans fight?" When, notwithstanding this, he was awarded the highest military decoration at the end of the war, he said, somewhat mischievously, that it was given "because he had not taken advantage by assuming power in Delhi. Is that not service enough?" The decoration arrived in a velvet case. Fateh Singh spurned to wear it on his honoured Rajput costume. "It's the sort of thing an attendant might wear", he said. "Put it on the horse. It looks better on a horse than on a king." Stories such as these may well be apocryphal, but that they should arise at all is eloquent testimony of the Maharana's attitude. What is certain is that when the Chamber of Princes was inaugurated in 1921 as a sop to princely participation in Imperial decisions, two rulers did not bother to attend: one was the Nizam of Hyderabad, the other Maharana Sir Fateh Singh of Udaipur.

In the same year, the Prince of Wales (later Edward VIII, still later Duke of Windsor) visited Udaipur. Fateh Singh did not receive him at the railway station. "He is the son of my respected and beloved brother by virtue of the treaty of friendship with him", he said. "He is like a son to me. Would you expect a father to receive his own son?" So he sent his son Bhupal to do the honours, claiming ill-health. Mr Holland, Agent to the Governor-General in Rajputana, wrote a secret letter to the British Government, which said, in part, "After much deliberation, I have come to the conclusion that the Maharana's illness was a deliberately planned affair, in order to escape going to the station to meet the Prince... In view of the fact that similar phenomena occurred on other occasions when the Maharana was expected to do something that he considered to be incongruous with his dignity, I think that he knows how to bring about a condition resembling serious disease of the heart in order to avoid the performance of some distasteful duty. I confess with disgust that I was wrong in believing him to be too much of a gentleman to resort to such a trick... It is difficult to say whether the Maharana's illness was feigned or not. If it was, His Highness evidently overdid it."

Fateh Singh contrived to recover quickly enough to pay a private visit to the Prince of Wales at the British Residency, when he presented him with a magnificent gun, and received in return a pair of stallions sent later from England. It was noticed that, on his return from the Residency to the City Palace, he acknowledged the salutations of people by the roadside for the first time in his life!

It was shortly after this that Fateh Singh's power was finally curtailed by the exasperated British. On 17 July, 1921, he was formally deposed, and though he was permitted to retain his titular right to the *gadi*, powers effectively devolved upon his son, Maharaj Kumar Bhupal Singh (Maharaj Kumar is a designation used by the heir-apparent). To be fair, it was not primarily his intractable pride of race which caused his demotion so much as an obdurate traditionalism which rendered him blind to social unrest in his State. He was totally out of touch with socialist movements which were gathering pace in the twentieth century—they were beyond his comprehension. He did not understand peasant disaffection, and therefore did nothing to appease it. He always acted in what he thought were the best interests of his people, as Curzon justly observed, but in his seventies he no longer intuited what those interests were. There was a danger that communist sympathies and lawlessness might spread in Mewar as a result of the Maharana's apparent instransigence.

Sir Fateh Singh lived for nine more years, frequently officiating as priest at the temple of Ekling ji. All differences were forgotten at his obsequies in 1930, when he was widely lamented as a great leader and a man of consummate nobility. It was as if a divinity had perished.

His mark is visible everywhere. He built a college in Udaipur, various schools and dispensaries sprinkled throughout the State, and a railway line to connect Udaipur with Chittor. He restored several old mansions in Chittor, and enlarged the Fateh Sagar lake with a canal to connect it with Lake Pichola; this and the Udai Sagar lake collect any overflow from Pichola, thus making it impossible for Udaipur to be flooded in case of excessive monsoon. (This was just as important a task as the construction of Lake Pichola itself by his ancestor Udai

Singh in the sixteenth century, so placed as to receive all water from mountains up to a hundred miles to the west.)

Fateh Singh restored the topmost summit of the palace at Kumbhalgarh, and occasionally resided there, and also built the Minto Durbar Hall, the impressive square building to the right of the fortress walls of the City Palace, when viewed from the lake, and in front of Shambhu Niwas Palace; it is now called Fateh Prakash. Finally, as we saw at the beginning, he completed the graceful Shiv Niwas Palace which curves round at the extreme right and is now a serenely peaceful hotel.

His most abiding memorial, however, is in the hearts of his people. A 95-year-old lady in the town gave the present author a vivid mental image of him, walking with a stick, a pure white turban on his head surrounded with a piece of black string to denote the premature passing of his daughter, distributing silver coins by dropping them into the outstretched *sari*s of the women. He was, she says with awe, "a saintly man, religious and pure."

Maharana Bhupal Singh seated with Sardar Vallabhbhai Patel and his daughter Maniben

Photograph by Prabhulal Verma, 14th–15th January, 1949
Acc. No. 2008.06.0474

INDEPENDENCE

Bhupal Singh was born in 1884, one year before his father's accession. (Fateh Singh had two other sons, who both died in infancy, as well as three daughters.) He would eventually enjoy the happy distinction of being the first son to succeed after an unbroken series of adoptions over the previous one hundred years. The happiness attending his birth and childhood was blighted, however, by the most cruel misfortune.

At the age of sixteen, Bhupal Singh contracted tuberculosis (not polio as is generally believed) and a disease called Pott's curvature of the spine. A projection of bone appeared at the back of his neck between his shoulders and grew rapidly, the protusion becoming unsightly after ten months. Unwilling to consult European doctors, the palace medical advisors allowed him to continue riding, with disastrous results. The tuberculosis spread to his lungs, and it was feared that he would not survive more than a month. His weight reduced to a scarcely credible three-and-a-half stone (50 lbs). Curzon sent a message of sympathy to his father. Fortunately, death was averted by timely intercession, but Bhupal never fully recovered. The disease left him paralysed from the waist down, confined to a wheelchair for the rest of his life, and denied him the satisfaction of his own progeny. His mind remained alert, and his spirit intact, which rendered the realisation of his disability all the harder to bear, especially as, of all the rulers of Mewar, he would have to live through the most momentous period since Pratap's heroic defence, and be called upon to make decisions of the utmost gravity during the revolutionary time when India came face to face with her destiny.

Bhupal Singh assumed ruling powers in 1921 and inherited the throne in 1930. Not once did he allow his crippled condition to impair his energies, and the early part of his reign was marked by real social advance. He governed from within the palace, rarely venturing out except for *shikar* (hunting wild game in the forests), when he was securely strapped to his horse. He was a kind and generous man, deeply concerned to relieve poverty and misery, at heart a liberal. At the same time, his Hindu philosophy was his source of strength, his piety his shield, and consciousness of his weighty responsibilities his pride.

Maharana Bhupal Singh was thrown into the thick of ferment and upheaval from the very beginning. Throughout the 1930s, as political awareness swept across the continent on that tide of enthusiasm which followed the great Mahatma Gandhi, the Maharana was bombarded with demands from a newly-vociferous people. A political party was formed, the Praja Mandal, to assert the rights of the masses and seek social improvements of hitherto unheard-of dimensions. From time to time, Bhupal Singh forbade demonstrations and marches and banished the more dangerous of the Praja Mandal spokesmen in his desire to avoid civil unrest. But the proscriptions were always reversed when calm had been restored. In 1932, an organised riot came right to the doors of Shambhu Niwas Palace. It was dispersed, and in their panic some of the rioters plunged into Lake Pichola. Bhupal sent his own boats to rescue them, and there were happily no casualties.

Inwardly, he felt a real sympathy with the people's aspirations, and sought, as far as he could, to indulge them. He was alive to the tenor of the times, and though he ruled over a state still mediaeval in some aspects of its social organisation, he was resolutely a man of the twentieth century in his intelligent appraisal of the need for drastic change. With his frustrating disability and the far-reaching consequences which attended his every word and deed, it is not fanciful to infer that he bore his mighty burden alone. In every photograph of him there is a sadness and weariness in the eyes which betoken constant worry; it is not a construct of the present writer's imagination—it is there for all to see.

Bhupal Singh set about securing the betterment of his people in his own way. He was a formidable educator, establishing the Rana Pratap Hindi University at Chittor, an Agricultural College at Udaipur, and schools by the dozen. Most significantly, he established a number of schools for the education of girls (the first school for girls had been built by Shambhu Singh in 1866). By 1940, he had increased literacy in his country ten-fold. He was again liberal in his support of religious communities, giving lavishly in cash and land to Christian, Sikh and Islamic foundations as well as Hindu ones.

His encouragement of economic advance was just as energetic. A special mining department was set up, with spectacular success in increased revenue. Sugar mills were built and industrial expansion encouraged. The finest example of Bhupal's vision was his attempt to arrest the denudation of forests. Aware of the ecological damage caused by wholesale destruction of trees, he brought in a forestry expert from Madras to formulate a long-sighted policy for their protection. Here, he was less successful, meeting with stiff opposition from vested interests and being unable to convince ordinary folk of the wisdom of leaving trees alone. (His attempt is all the more laudable in the light of what happened after his death; no sooner had the Indian government appropriated Mewar lands in the 1970s, than they chopped down everything in sight, leaving the Aravalli hills irreversibly barren, with disastrous consequences to the climate.)

It is for his role in the Independence of India and the formation of the Rajasthan Union that Bhupal Singh will inevitably be chiefly remembered. It should be made clear that India, as a corporate uniform identity, had never existed in history. Geographically, it was a vast sub-continent composed of a multitude of different countries, peoples, and languages. Under the British, it had been divided into two parts: on the one hand, British India, directly administered from London; and on the other, hundreds of independent States of various sizes, together accounting for nearly one-third of the entire territory, bound to Britain by the treaties of 1818 and subject to a certain amount of supervision by Political Agents or Residents. As Hugh Davenport has graphically put it, "Up to 17 April, 1948, Maharana Bhupal Singh of Udaipur, Mewar had his own army, police force, judiciary, educational system, and day to day governance of his kingdom." Fate decreed that he should be the one to sign all this away, and he confronted this fate with both dignity and resolve.

The Socialist government in England under Clement Attlee decided in 1945 that Great Britain should withdraw totally from India at the earliest possible moment, and Lord Mountbatten was sent out as last Viceroy to make speedy arrangements for the transference of power. To hand over British India was a comparatively easy matter. But the Princely States presented a different problem. Was not Britain bound to honour treaties negotiated in good faith? Apparently not. Had not Queen Victoria promised to protect the dignity and independence of the States "as Our own"? Even that undertaking was not eternal. A cabinet mission sent from London in 1946 made it clear that "political arrangements between the States on one side and the British Crown and British India on the other will thus be brought to an end." In other words, the treaties were to be abrogated, and the rulers would simply have to accept the fact. Their sovereignty would have to be surrendered "voluntarily" to the new Indian government.

The rulers were in hopeless disarray. Winston Churchill counted on their banding together in a powerful federation to resist the socialist plans (echoing once more Maharana Pratap's unbending defence of liberty), but the rulers, never very good at concerted action, dithered, prevaricated, and could not make up their minds. Old-fashioned Indian lethargy set in, and they waited supinely for their countries to be wiped off the map.

Well, not entirely. In the forefront of attempts to work out a united policy was Bhupal Singh of Udaipur, Mewar. More than once he brought other rulers to Udaipur to discuss possible responses to the British proposals. To the ruler of Alwar he wrote, "Last year I invited here several Highnesses to consider this question but without producing any result. Only one or two rulers did relish the idea of combined action. Rulers have been meeting and discussing but they are afraid of taking decisive action." Some British politicians were urging the princes to refuse allegiance to the new independent India, with the ignoble intention that chaos would ensue and Britain would be summoned to return and resume Imperial authority. Some princes entertained the equally vain hope that the principle of Paramountcy could be retained, with an Indian supervising power replacing the British one and internal independence of the Princely States retained. Bhupal Singh immediately discerned that both attitudes were against the tide of national feeling and therefore, in the widest sense, unpatriotic. He would not lend his name to either approach. With a ringing display of firmness, he declared, "My choice was made by my ancestors. If they had faltered they would have left us a kingdom as large as Hyderabad. They did not. Neither will I. I am with India."

"The next day", wrote the eminent constitutionalist K.M. Munshi, "one of the Maharana's ministers telephoned me in Delhi to inform me about the Maharana's statement. I replied that I was filled with admiration for it. Nothing could be nobler, and this too on the eve of the almost certain extinction of his 1500-year-old dynastic rule."

It was the turning point as far as the Princely States were concerned. In their indecent haste to force decisions, the British were pushing the clock forward at a grotesque pace. Time was running out. Rulers were given until 15 August 1947 to sign their adherence to either India or Pakistan. In July, Mountbatten urged them to hurry, "The States are theoretically free to link their future with whichever dominion they may care", he said. "But when I say that they are at liberty to link up with either of the dominions, may I point out that there are certain geographical compulsions which cannot be evaded. Out of something like 565 States, the vast majority are irretrievably linked geographically with the dominion of India. Remember that the day of transference of power is very close at hand, and if you are prepared to come, you must come before 15 August." It is difficult to see how this could be construed as anything else but a gun firmly placed behind the neck.

Nehru and Gandhi likewise added their word of warning. Personally, with his solid sense of history, Nehru admired Bhupal both for his integrity and for the incomparable nobility of his forebears. But politics were harsh. "We will not recognise any independence for any State in India", he said with categorical emphasis. "Further, recognition of such independence by any foreign power, whichever it may be and wherever it may be, will be considered an unfriendly act." For his part, Mahatma Gandhi said that if the princes affirmed independence, it would be "tantamount to a declaration of war against the free millions of India."

In the face of such universal concurrence of opinion, continued resistance would have been the most irresponsible folly. Bhupal Singh took the lead, and made Mewar the first State to merge with the Indian Union, thus putting an end to a sovereignty founded by Guhil in the sixth century and proudly defended against countless incursions ever since. What had endured for nearly 1500 years had taken only a matter of months to dismantle and that without a shot being fired. The emotional shock was tremendous. When the Maharaja of Dhrangadhra announced the dissolution of his country and assured his people that it had been done in their interest, one old man who heard him, said, "That is all very well, Sir, I know what you have done. But who will now wipe away our tears?"

There are two views of Bhupal Singh's capitulation. One is that he betrayed his ancestry by being the first ruler in the history of Mewar to give in to foreign coercion. This was more or less the substance of a jibe made by the Prime Minister of Bikaner, who said that the Maharana's forefathers had been the last of the Rajput princes to bow before the Moghuls, yet he was the first to bow before the Congress. To this, Bhupal Singh, who was privately hurt and distressed, replied that postponement would have promised neither better conditions nor better rewards.

The alternative holds that Bhupal acted in a manner entirely consistent with his family's subservience to the deity Ekling ji, in whose name he is bound to serve the interests and welfare of his people. Just as his ancestors had not bowed to the Turkish Sultans, or to the Moghul Emperors, or to the British Monarchy, because they each threatened foreign usurpation of Ekling ji's god-given right to rule, so Bhupal Singh did not bow to Ekling ji's enemies, but to Ekling ji himself. If he ruled only on behalf of the people, then he must respect the democratic ideal expressed by the people, and in so doing he continued to serve Ekling ji's will.

And so it was with confidence, not shame, that the Maharana was able to deliver his historic speech on the occasion of India's creation as a free country. "Today is a day of which to be greatly proud", he said. "India is independent. It brings to fulfillment the 1400 years' struggle and endeavour of my forefathers. It becomes my holy duty, on behalf of my ancestors, to hand over to the leaders of free India, this cherished and sacred Flame of Freedom, to the country as a whole."

This was what Pratap and Sanga had fought for all along. Theirs was the final triumph.

One thing is certain. By his timely and statesmanlike decision, Bhupal avoided schism and disruption in Rajasthan. So intense was the respect in which the Mewar dynasty was held, that his lead was followed and a smooth transfer of power effected. What was good enough for the Maharana of Udaipur was good enough for them all.

Two years later, the Union of Greater Rajasthan came into being. Although he was first in rank and dignity among Rajput princes, Bhupal Singh could not easily be made Rajpramukh of Rajasthan because the wheelchair restricted his movements. A special position was created for him, that of Maharajpramukh, to hold precedence over the Rajpramukh on all ceremonial occasions as a kind of titular Head of the Union, the position to be held for his lifetime only, and not to devolve upon his heirs.

From the Shivrati branch of the family (the same which had produced Maharana Fateh Singh), Bhupal had adopted as his son, in 1939, Bhagwat Singh, another lineal descendant of Sangram II, and in fact Fateh Singh's great-nephew.

Incidentally, the nature of adoption in India is frequently misunderstood by foreigners. In the West, it is not uncommon for an adopted child to refer to his natural family as well as his adopted family, effectively making him the 'child' of both. The custom in India is radically different. Once the adoption has been effected, the child is surrendered totally to his new circumstances, exactly as if his original parents had no connection with him. In this way, Bhagwat was the son of Bhupal and grandson of Fateh in law and in fact, not in theory.

Bhupal's sagacity and foresight are attested by an act he made in favour of Bhagwat shortly after the adoption. Knowing full well that democracy was an ideal which could be traduced if consigned to the wrong hands, he made over to his son the palaces of Shiv Niwas and Shambhu Niwas absolutely, to be inalienable from him and his heirs. (This act remained secret for many years.) To this day, both palaces are legally protected, and as far as one can predict, cannot be expropriated by any future Indian government.

Bhupal Singh died in 1955.

MAHARANA KUMBHA.

Rana Kumbha (1433–1468)

Painted by Chaturbhuj

Acc. No. 2010.T.0004

Rana Pratap (1572–1597)
Painted by Raja Ravi Varma, 1901
Acc. No. 2011.T.0021

Maharana Shambhu Singh (1861–1874)

Maharana Sajjan Singh (1874–1884)
Painted by Shiva Lal
Acc. No. 2008.07.0272_R

FACING PAGE **Maharana Fateh Singh (1884–1930)**
Painted by Raja Ravi Varma, 1901
Acc. No. 2011.T.0020

Maharana Bhagwat Singh (1955–1984)

Painted by B.G. Sharma, 1995
Acc. No. 2011.T.0022

Shriji Arvind Singh Mewar of Udaipur (1984)

Lakshyaraj Singh Mewar of Udaipur with his mother Vijayraj Kumari Mewar of Udaipur
Photograph by Himanshu Pahad

INTO THE FUTURE

Bhagwat Singh had been brought up fairly conventionally in a small family, went as an ordinary schoolboy to an ordinary school, and enjoyed his free time in sport with his two younger brothers, Narendra Singh and Arjun Singh. When he was seventeen, he could not help noticing that certain strangers were taking an undue interest in his progress, were lurking about, checking up on him. What he could not know was that he was undergoing the process of inspection before he was formally adopted as son and heir to the Maharana.

We are fortunate in that Bhagwat Singh has left us his own memoirs, unpublished, of these days, affording us for the first time an inside account of what it was like to be transmuted from a humble schoolboy to an august prince.

On his first day at the palace he was astonished to discover that he was surrounded by hundreds of people all the time, and was expected to take the encumbrance in his stride. His first meal was a luncheon, cemented in formality, at which he was required to eat his meal while one hundred courtiers sat watching him, their plates empty. Not surprisingly, his appetite failed him. The rest of the day was marked by ceremonial presentations and precise rituals which quite wore him out. He was happy to be shown to his private quarters for the night.

Even there he was denied the solace of solitude. Four men stood at the foot of his bed as he tried to sleep. They were relieved every two hours. In this detail, nothing had changed since the days of Fateh Singh, who also was watched in slumber every night of his reign. Bhagwat was not prepared for it. He did not sleep for five minutes, and the following day was weak with fatigue. He felt frightened and trapped, and could foresee only a miserable existence of gorgeous imprisonment. He begged that the formality should be reduced. So, when his companions at mealtimes were allowed to eat in his presence, and the guards were removed to a position outside his bedroom door, his terror abated. To help him adapt, permission was granted for him to visit his natural family at the weekend, in a more relaxed atmosphere.

The following year, at the age of nineteen, he was married to a Bikaner princess. Again, he had no idea the marriage was being planned or a wife chosen for him. He had not met her before. Ten thousand people were involved in the three-day festivities, plus a whole army unit and herds of elephants. Two thousand people made the journey by train from Udaipur to Bikaner. But nobody thought to tell Bhagwat what a knife and fork were for (such instruments had still not been introduced at court in Udaipur), nor how to deal with married life. The latter, of course, was not yet important. After the wedding, Maharaj Kumar Bhagwat Singh went back to school. At Mayo College, a few months later, he was served by a retinue of twelve men who accompanied him from Udaipur.

By the time of his accession in 1955, Bhagwat was the father of two sons and a daughter. If he confessed, on the eve of his enthronement, to a certain apprehension about the onus he was about to take on, his subsequent career was to demonstrate his determination to respect the legacy of Bappa Rawal despite severely altered circumstances.

The Prime Minister of India, Jawaharlal Nehru, knew the value of all historical gesture. In 1956 he invited the Maharana of Udaipur to visit the Red Fort at Delhi. Bhagwat Singh readily accepted. The symbolic import of both the invitation and the acceptance was not lost on Indians. It was gracious of Nehru to seek the Maharana's presence in Delhi; he certainly had no personal or political necessity to do so. But he knew that successive Maharanas had resolutely upheld the ancient vow of their family never to enter Delhi so long

Bhagwat Singh at the time of his marriage, 1939. On the left, his father Maharana Bhupal Singh, on the right, his guardian Captain Harvey Jones

Photograph by K.L. Syed & Co.
Acc. No. 2008.08.0091

as it remained in the hands of a foreign power. Now that at last it was governed by Indians, the Maharana was able to fulfill that promise. The effect of his visit was a powerful inspiration to free India, an endorsement of the supreme prize of Independence.

(Incidentally, one may reasonably question the logic of adherence to this vow. After three hundred years of occupation, the Moghul emperors had some right to claim that they were as much "Indian" as anyone else; Akbar certainly considered himself so to be. But such pedantry ignores the significance of an emotional commitment.)

In the same year, the Maharana began seriously to ponder the future. At the time of Independence the rulers had been given a solemn undertaking by the government: though they relinquished their sovereignty, they would retain their titles and palaces and receive a Privy Purse from public funds in recognition of the amalgamation of that sovereignty into the greater sovereignty of India. The Privy Purse would have the additional advantage of supplanting the internal state revenues which had disappeared and would help maintain the palaces. The cost of preventing the City Palace from crumbling was however formidable, and Bhagwat Singh therefore decided that supplementary funds would need to be found to ensure survival of the buildings. He established a private company to which he sold the Lake Palace (Jagniwas), the island of Jagmandir, the palace known as Fateh Prakash (which contains the Durbar Hall), and certain lands on the shore of the lake beneath the City Palace. These thereupon ceased to be his private property. He then set about adapting (not "converting") the ravishing Lake Palace to serve as a luxury hotel. It opened amid clamorous publicity in 1963, and has remained ever since one of the world's most desirable holiday accommodations.

The success of the Lake Palace venture allowed the Maharana to feel secure in the provisions he had made for the generations to follow him, and in the light of this he made over to his eldest son, Mahendra Singh, the mansion and surrounding acres known as Samore Gardens. Mahendra Singh disputes this, maintaining that the house is still Joint Family property. The house and garden may be seen from the heights of Shiv Niwas Palace, lying just below.

It was also in Bhagwat Singh's time that Queen Elizabeth II paid a visit to Udaipur and was received as a guest at Shiv Niwas. When he naturally offered the Queen precedence, she demurred, saying, "Please lead the way. You come from a much older family than I do!" A few months later Jacqueline Kennedy, wife of the President of the United States, also stayed at Shiv Niwas. Bhagwat himself became the first Maharana ever to go abroad; his predecessors had for the most part not strayed beyond the boundaries of Mewar.

Then, in 1969, the Indian government dealt a terrible blow. In contravention of the undertakings made at the time of Independence and the voluntary fusion of the Princely States with the Indian Union, undertakings moreover guaranteed by the Constitution of India, Parliament decided that the rulers should be deprived of their vestigial privileges, stripped of their titles, and robbed of their Privy Purses. This time the erstwhile rulers did not concede by default. A Concord of Princes was formed to contest the 1969 legislation and present a reasoned objection to the Supreme Court. Meanwhile, Bhagwat Singh wrote in polite but anguished terms to the Prime Minister, Indira Gandhi, in a letter which must be regarded as a perfect example of the dignity with which the House of Mewar has always striven to protect its hereditary duty. Mrs Gandhi had requested that the Maharana "assist the government in doing away with certain institutions", without any intention "to cause hardship to the Rulers or to injure their self-respect." Part of his reply is reproduced here:

> The settlements made between the Rulers and the Union were brought about honourably and with responsibility... If what was thus settled is now unsettled by Government there is no gainsaying that we would be treated like aliens in our own Motherland.
>
> You are not unaware of the affection and trust with which we are treated by the people in our own areas. Indeed you have alluded to

it. Were it not for this love and confidence in us and our tradition of service, we would have ceased to exist long ago. But in point of fact it is this continuing relationship of reciprocal love which appears to be the reason why we and our institutional being is disliked by some politicians.

I need not tell you that the institution of Maharana has a history of fourteen centuries behind it, a history which is universally admitted as glorious and unsullied. I am merely its trustee and servant, for such a time as it pleases God. Please consider, please reflect for a moment, whether I would deserve to live, whether those who value history and traditions would own me as an Indian, if I were to acquiesce in the derogation of this institution. It is not my private possession. It belongs to the people. If the traditions created by the people of Mewar, or of any other place, are not preserved, what will there be left to inspire the nation and invigorate our self-reliance, self-respect, and integrity?

Having said this, having personal regard for your esteemed father [Nehru], and trusting in your sincerity, let me assure you that you may ask for any sacrifice from me in person, and it shall be an honour for me to be of service to the country, save only that I cannot accept to be instrumental in any derogation of the institution to which I belong. You have referred to hardship. Well, hardships are to be endured, but not dishonour.

Sadly, the plea was to no avail. Lest the Supreme Court should rule that the government proposals were unconstitutional, Parliament re-wrote the Constitution, and finally, by the Constitutional Amendment Act of 1971, the rulers became ordinary citizens of the democratic Republic and their privileges and allowances ceased forthwith. From now on, they would have to fend for themselves, and seek whatever income they might. That the maintenance of the huge palaces was a weight henceforth to be borne without any assistance was of no concern to anyone. After their betrayal by the departing British, it was the second major adaptation they were required to face within twenty-five years.

The most important aspect of this legislation was symbolic. The rulers were degraded by the abrupt removal of that respect which they had earned through centuries of service. They would no longer be exempt from criminal prosecution (thereby insinuating that they were potentially capable of criminal acts) and would no longer be provided with a guard of honour (thus underlining that their honour did not deserve recognition). They would also be liable to estate duty like anyone else, and their palaces became, at a stroke, a taxable asset of probably ruinous proportions. There were many who thought the government was, with no visible cause, spiteful and vindictive.

That he should be known by the Indian equivalent of "Mr Mewar" frankly caused Bhagwat Singh no perturbation of spirit. His worries were rather, on the one hand, how to make practical commercial use of the buildings, on the other, how to continue a cherished tradition.

On the practical side, he had already given the City Palace to the government, which had promptly dispersed the contents. Realising that it was being mismanaged, he had recovered it intact, a huge gamble in view of the liability it threatened to represent, In 1969, Bhagwat Singh established a charitable trust to which he donated the main portions of the City Palace (*mardana* and *zenana*), together with what was left of their contents, as well as a considerable endowment. The trust was called the Maharana of Mewar Charitable Foundation. Its funds derive both from interest on the original endowment and from entrance fees to the City Palace Complex, now a museum open to the public.

He also added another floor to Shiv Niwas Palace and transformed it into a luxury hotel, for which purpose another private company was formed. Shiv Niwas is leased to this company in perpetuity.

As to the more fundamental, intangible matter of how to continue a philosophic ideal, Bhagwat made two crucial decisions at different points in his life. First, he decreed that monies earned by the Maharana of Mewar Charitable Foundation should be devoted to social welfare and education, in consideration of his belief that the family's long record of work for the benefit of the community must not be interrupted, and he appointed trustees who would uphold this principle. Behind this intention lay firm adherence to the instructions of Maharishi Harit Rashi, who gave the State of Mewar in trust to Bappa Rawal seventy-five generations before, to administer in the name of Ekling ji. Although there was no longer any State to administer or defend, the population was still there, and the great majority of them were descendants of the original subjects under Bappa Rawal's rule. One of the guiding principles vouchsafed by Maharishi Harit Rashi to Bappa and his progeny was to keep the human soul in a state of alertness, in order that human beings should value the dignity of Man. Another was that self-reliance and self-respect should on no account be compromised.

In compliance with such precepts, the Maharana of Mewar Charitable Foundation instituted a number of financial awards to be granted annually for services of a permanent value rendered to society. They include awards for historical research, art and painting, music and dance, education and journalism, and a variety of other contributions to social welfare, and they are now prized and famous throughout India. In addition, the Foundation set up a number of subsidiary trusts for religious and charitable purposes, to give assistance without distinction of caste, creed or religion in the honoured tradition of a family which has never descended to bigotry. One of these, the Vidyadan Trust (which means the Charity of Knowledge) now runs the secondary school which is part of the City Palace Complex.

Bhagwat Singh's second decision came long after the passing of the Constitutional Amendment Act of 1971, which purported to put an end to the lineage of Maharanas. This was a fate he could not envisage with equanimity, and he resolved to counter it in a novel and interesting manner. Since the Maharana no longer existed as a legal entity, he determined to discover a way in which the institution of Maharana could continue and still be legally and socially acceptable. He reflected upon this for many years, until he devised the solution in 1984 and incorporated it in his last Will and Testament.

Since future generations would not succeed to the style of Maharana, and since within half a century or less the very name of Maharana might become a mere historical fossil, Bhagwat recreated the institution of Maharana by his Will. He directed that all his remaining assets, including Shambhu Niwas Palace, be donated to a new Trust, to be called the Maharana Mewar Institution Trust, of which the Managing Trustee should be his second son, Arvind Singh. Thus, though legally his chosen heir might not be called Maharana, he would still be guardian of the institution of Maharana, legally constituted, and the name of Maharana would continue in perpetuity. By this far-sighted device, he ensured that the Maharanas would not terminate with the seventy-fifth generation, but would continue under another guise. For the first seventy-five generations, the institution was invested in a person, an individual; henceforth it would be vested in a Trust. Fittingly, as it began with a trust pledged to Bappa Rawal, so it may forever remain a trust, pledged to his descendants.

A few months after making this Will, Bhagwat Singh died suddenly at the age of sixty-three, a day-and-a-half after the assassination of Indira Gandhi. The combination of events was shattering to the people of Udaipur, who poured up to the City Palace to pay their respects to the last man legally entitled to be their Maharana, and lined the streets in their thousands for his obsequies.

When the Will was read, it was found to contain not only the establishment of the new Trust already referred to, but an unequivocal disapproval of the elder son, Maharaj Kumar Mahendra Singh. Mahendra had displeased his father by filing a lawsuit against him which sought to partition the family inheritance in accordance with a provision of the ancient Hindu law known as the Hindu

Undivided Family. By this act, Mahendra is understood to have voluntarily seceded from the family, which he no longer regarded as one indivisible unit. Mulla's *Principles of Hindu Law** is quite clear on the matter. Paragraph 325 discusses how partition may be effected. "All that is necessary.... to constitute a partition is a definite and unequivocal indication of his intention by a member of a joint family to separate himself from the family and enjoy his share in severalty." This indication of intention takes effect immediately and is irrevocable. One way in which the intention may be made manifest is by the institution of a suit for partition. Mahendra Singh filed just such a Civil Suit in 1983, and by this act would, in law, sever himself from any Joint Family to which he had previously belonged.

The idea of splitting the family into equal parts was anathema to Bhagwat Singh, for he reasoned that the Maharana cannot be fragmented in this way, and what the Maharana represents, more than anything, is unity of purpose and respect for a duty which cannot be abnegated.

Mahendra's objection was that his father had wilfully disposed of many family possessions in his lifetime, thereby depriving him of some of his rightful inheritance. It is a view which does not take account of Bhagwat's deeply-set motives. To uphold the ancient ideal of service to the community, the various trusts had to be endowed with cash. Jewellery, garments and furniture can be of no benefit to society, only to the individual who possesses them, and the Mewar dynasty has never placed much value on personal possessions or ownership as such. He espoused the view that one comes into this life with nothing, and takes nothing out, and that therefore to place reliance on acquisition of goods, or their retention, was an absurdity.

Bhagwat Singh was convinced that his elder son Mahendra did not share this view, and was unlikely ever to share it. Such, at least, is the purport of

---

* Sir Dinshah Fardunji Mulla, *Principles of Hindu Law* (1952)

paragraphs in his Will wherein he states clearly that "setting aside my personal emotions as a father", he must debar his elder son from the succession on very specific grounds. "I visualise that the Institution of Maharana, the name of the family and the various Trusts and responsibilities attached to it", he wrote, "will not be safe in the hands of Maharaj Kumar Mahendra Singh."

The decision caused some initial consternation and bewilderment in the city, where the full circumstances of what had preceded it were not widely appreciated, or were in some cases energetically suppressed. In fact, Bhagwat Singh had little choice in the matter, since, as has been clearly stated above, Mahendra Singh having voluntarily and unequivocally severed himself from the family forever, there was no possibility of his being in the line of succession. Nevertheless, the Will was contested, unsuccessfully, raising yet another point of legality.

As stated above, if the Mewar dynasty had been a Joint Hindu Family, then Mahendra Singh severed himself from that family in 1983. If, however, it was not, what then would apply? The Mewar dynasty has never, in fact, been a Joint Hindu Family, and its property has always been regarded as ancestral and therefore an "impartible" estate, (i.e. incapable of partition or division). It passes down the generations from father to son and has been inherited by each Maharana in turn. The question was, now that there was no longer any legal force to the concept of one person being "Maharana", could the estate be disposed of by Will in contravention of the rules of primogeniture, which are a salient feature of an impartible estate? Since Mahendra Singh had no "title" to inherit, all that was left was the property; could this be denied him by the Will of his father?

The Supreme Court of India made a historic ruling in a similar case at the beginning of 1988 (Case No.247). The holder of an impartible Raj estate (i.e. the estate of a former ruler), has, said the Court, an unlimited power of alienation not only by transfer *inter vivos* but also by will, even if this defeats the rights of

Baadi Mahal at The City Palace Museum

survivorship or primogeniture. In other words, the former ruler may do what he likes with his property.

Bhagwat Singh's Will was decreed by the courts to be a sound and valid expression of his wishes. As a result, and in accordance with those wishes, the acting head of the family and modern representative of the seed of Bappa Rawal is the second son, previously known as Maharaj Kumar Arvind Singh ("MK Sahib" for short). It is he who manages the Trusts, he who runs the hotels, and he who pays homage to Ekling ji, as his ancestors have done before him, every Monday evening.

Moreover, Arvind Singh has added to the list of awards made by the Maharana of Mewar Charitable Foundation a highly significant one bestowed for services to national integration. It is significant because it is called the Hakim Khan Sur Award, named after the man who led Rana Pratap's troops at the battle of Haldi Ghati in 1576, and the reader will recall that Hakim was not a Hindu fighting for Hindus, but a Pathan (Muslim) fighting for all. The name of this award therefore underlines yet again the unwavering devotion of this dynasty, throughout the centuries, to the notion of religious tolerance in the name of freedom.

Arvind Singh Mewar is married to the grand-daughter of the ruler of Kutch, Princess Vijayraj, and they have two daughters and a son. The daughters have married and moved away from Udaipur. Bhargavi, the elder now lives in Jaipur. The marriage of the younger, Padmaja, in 2011, was the occasion of a glorious celebration according to the ancient traditional customs of Mewar, lasting several days and in preparation for many months. Nothing like it had been seen in Udaipur for half a century, and the whole town participated. The son and heir, Lakshyaraj, resides with his parents in the palace of Shambhu Niwas, within the City Palace Complex.

Two further matters deserve attention. This is not the first time that the honour of the style "Maharana" has passed not to the first-born, but to a younger son.

It happened in the fourteenth century, when Chunda voluntarily relinquished such right in favour of his half-brother Mokal. But this presupposes that the style of Maharana might still be said to exist, despite modern legislation. Which brings us to the second point.

"Maharana" is not so much a title as an honorary style of address conferred by the people of Mewar upon their ruler and representative before God. As such, since it was never granted by any one mortal authority, neither can it be removed by any one authority. To understand this concept, it is instructive to contrast it with that which applies in England, where the fount of all honour and titles is the Crown. What the Crown bestows, it may also withdraw. Hence a dukedom, a marquessate or a viscountcy is hereditary in the family of the grantee until such time as the Crown may cancel it by Attainder. This happened to the Duke of Monmouth in 1685, and the title is still in abeyance unless the Crown removes the Attainder. It also happened to more than one Duke of Norfolk, with subsequent restoration by the monarch. The Maharana is not the holder of a title in this sense at all. His is sovereign, the giver of titles. The style of Maharana can only be removed by the people, and it may be said that this is precisely what happened by vote in Parliament in 1971. But the people of Mewar were not consulted on that occasion, and those among them who still wish to regard their chief as "Maharana" cannot be prevented from so doing, any more than the present writer may cease to be styled "Mr". By this reckoning, the 76th head of the House of Mewar, though no longer a ruler, is Maharana Arvind Singh.

He carries in his genes the mark of an extraordinary history. Though some of the stories relating to the earliest centuries may smack of fantasy and be legendary in their detail, they start from a specific event and are then expanded by bardic embellishment to allegorical proportions, as a source of inspiration to the people. Still, the epic scale of their well-attested achievements is not open to doubt. We shall leave the final word with the historian G.H. Ojha, whose *History of Udaipur State* is definitive:

In the past 1400 years, hundreds of ancient States have perished, many new States were founded, the fortunes of India have undergone many vicissitudes. Hundreds of princes have bowed before the might of the Imperial Powers at Delhi and surrendered their honour, traditions and dignity at their feet, but the ruling family of Udaipur, which is the oldest ruling family in the world, has not deviated from its path of firmly maintaining its honour and traditions unimpaired in spite of suffering innumerable hardships, undergoing untold dangers, and sacrificing wealth and worldly comforts. It is because of this that India looks upon the Maharanas with respect and calls them "Sun of the Hindus".

THE CONCEPT OF CUSTODIAN

Throughout this book there has been frequent reference to the notion that the rulers of Mewar have been for fourteen centuries no more than representatives, humble guardians of a trust vested in them in perpetuity, a trust, moreover, bearing exigent duties and responsibilities towards the people and the land. Arvind Singh Mewar is no longer a ruler in the strict legal sense, but his inherited duties and responsibilities cannot be voted away by mere shuffling of laws; they are total, binding, and everlasting, and he feels their potency with a profound sense of piety. Why? Because the true ruler of this land is Shree Eklingnath ji, the family deity and manifestation of the god Shiva, and he, Arvind Singh Mewar, is custodian of the land on behalf of that deity, and remains so regardless of changes in the political situation. He puts it in this way: "The very fact that sovereignty of Mewar rests in a deity helps us stay humble and grounded. We are not the owners, but the custodians of the state of Mewar, who are supposed to be serving, protecting and growing the kingdom in our lifetime and then passing it on to the next generation."

This concept of a "custodian" is difficult to grasp in a modern democracy; it appears so remote and antiquated, whereas in truth, it is the very reverse, for it treads a steady path well into the future in despite of the vagaries of political fortune. It has endured because it is greater, and indeed simpler, than any ordinary system of governance invented by men. It is at the root of honour, and it is as much felt as it is observed.

We shall here attempt to explain this concept and then demonstrate its practical results. Its relevance was thrown into stark reality by the publicity surrounding the discovery in 2011 of a vast treasure of gold stored in the vaults beneath a temple in the former kingdom of Travancore within the state of what is today Kerala. The trove has still not been properly valued, and perhaps it never will, but any sensible estimate stretches into the billions of dollars. The Supreme Court directed a team to take stock of what was there; one of them, Justice Rajan, said, "I have never seen such a sight in my life, it is magnificent." Suddenly, a temple, mostly unknown to the outside world, became the world's richest, in theory. That is what claimed the world's breathless attention. Money was what mattered. But not so to the former ruler of Travancore, whose ancestors had donated the treasure over gradual centuries to the family deity, and then forgotten about it. Beguilingly, this man, Marthanda Verma, told how, once at a game reserve in South Africa, he had asked which was the most rapacious and fearsome animal, and had been shown a mirror. It was a moment of piercing truth. And yet he himself was indifferent to wealth; "We did not get gobbled up by Western thought", he said.

The immediate and, in some ways, natural response of many English people was that the temple riches should be turned into cash and put to useful purpose for the benefit of the local population; no limit to the roads, hospitals and schools that could be funded with such bounty. Marthanda Verma was politely and sweetly dismissive of such an idea. "Please don't remove those objects from the temple", he said. "They belong to nobody, certainly not to our family." An English visitor has only to reflect upon what might be the fate of our own Crown Jewels housed beneath the Tower of London for hundreds of years. They do not belong to the Queen; she merely wears some of them from time to time, and they are always returned to the Tower. Anyone who suggested that they should be sold off and used by the Treasury for whatever spending purpose politicians might devise would be laughed to scorn. Why, then, suggest that the Kerala temple's riches could be better used, while maintaining that the British Crown Jewels must be left where they are? This is not just double standards—it smacks of resurgent colonialism.

The point of the story is that Travancore and Udaipur share similar traditions of custodianship. It is perhaps no coincidence that they are the oldest dynasties on the sub-continent of India, for such tenacious ideas only strengthen with antiquity. Udaipur's ruling family traces their duty as custodians to the year 734, Travancore's to the year 820, with less than a century between them. The Maharanas regarded themselves as *dewan*s or servants of the deity Ekling ji; the kings of Travancore considered themselves *dasa*s (devotees) of the deity Padmanabha; 'dewan' and 'dasa' may be translated by the modern 'custodian', whose individual identity is wholly subsumed by the need to serve. Says Marthanda Verma: "When you are trustee, chairman, benefactor or president, your personality is still there. In this, nothing is there, you are nobody. You carry on your duty." And on the parallel with Udaipur: "the king goes to the Ekling ji temple as a Maharana, but enters the shrine as a servant. A servant can resign his job, but a *dasa* (custodian) can do so only when he dies."

We have heard the word 'custodian' applied to similar situations in other countries. One is reminded of Elizabeth II's solemn declaration, as Princess Elizabeth on her 21st birthday broadcast. "Whether my life be long or short" she said, "it shall be devoted to your service." Thus did she espouse her duty as custodian of the people's sovereignty during her lifetime.

The most salient point of this comparison is, however, that the British constitutional monarchy is a relatively new concept, still in its infancy when made to stand alongside the principle of custodianship established by Bappa Rawal in 734. The House of Mewar was founded while Europe was still struggling to emerge from primitive lawlessness, and even long before the idea that monarchs ruled by divine right became the accepted norm in France, in Britain, in Russia and elsewhere. The British monarchy matured eventually, and spurned the divine right assumption of absolute power at the end of the seventeenth century, finally settling into a form of governance which uncannily resembled the principle of custodianship which had prevailed in Mewar for already one thousand years. Hence Bappa Rawal was prescient by centuries, and the British monarchy, unknowingly, followed a long-revered example set as precedent on a distant continent.

Of course, it would be unwise to press the comparisons too far, but the very act of bringing together two distinct forms of governance into one sentence helps to elucidate the key value of each. All human societies resemble one another more or less, but it is always their stark differences that most readily spring to notice. Scratch away the details which differentiate one from the other, and their underlying similarities shine forth with astonishing clarity.

The British constitutional monarchy offers more instances worth pondering in the light of Mewar's history. Once a year, Queen Elizabeth II presides over the State Opening of Parliament in October; her role on that occasion is to read from the throne her government's legislative programme for the coming session. She has nothing to do with its drafting and makes no input to its content; she simply reads it out aloud. But the important symbolism lies in the Imperial State Crown which she wears for that occasion, once every year.

The Queen arrives at the Houses of Parliament with great pomp and ceremony, in a golden horse-driven coach preceded by a regiment of her personal guards on horseback. She is greeted by the Lord Great Chamberlain and escorted, with her husband Prince Philip, up the long Sovereign's Staircase to the robing-room. Meanwhile, the Imperial State Crown has arrived separately, brought there in advance under escort from the Tower of London. Between the robing-room and the House of Lords where the throne awaits her is the Royal Gallery with three rows of seats on either side. Here sit approximately 300 spectators who are there by invitation; these are not officials, they are simply people, citizens, her subjects, but nevertheless present by right, as it is their Parliament and their democracy that they will witness at work. The Crown is brought in and placed on a cushion on a simple square table in the middle of the long room, alone and unattended, for all of us to stare at. It is there because it is ours; it represents the sovereignty of the people. It is then taken to the robing-room, and minutes later, trumpets sound, doors fling open, and the Queen walks along the entire room, her long ermine train behind her and the crown upon her head. It is not hers by right; she wears it as a symbol of her position as head of state in whose name government exercises its authority. She is, at that moment, the *custodian* of that sovereignty which belongs to the people, and her duty is to care for the people by representing their interests. She has none of her own. She is there to serve. Service lies at the heart of monarchy as it has grown over the centuries in Britain. And afterwards, the crown goes back to the Tower of London until we call for it again.

It is helpful for a British reader to see why the custody of the crown, symbol of the people's well-being, matters to us, the better to understand why the custodianship of the people and land of Mewar matters to Udaipur where it has prevailed for much longer. Arvind Singh Mewar is the 76th such custodian in unbroken succession; Elizabeth II is the 13th since the constitutional monarchy was established to replace the divine right of kings in 1688. (It may be noted that in Britain, although the principle of service has obtained since mediaeval times, it was only in 1688 that its constitutional dynamic was clarified.)

Another useful illustration might be derived from an examination of the ritual of the Queen's coronation at Westminster Abbey in 1953. We have already seen that the spiritual element of custodianship is central to Mewar in that the true ruler is held to be the deity Ekling ji, on whose behalf the Maharanas have protected and served the people. So too does the coronation ceremony reveal in dramatic and poetic fashion the spiritual element of the British monarch's duty towards her people. It is, after all, a profoundly religious ceremony. At the moment of Elizabeth's anointing in 1953, there stood a young woman of twenty-six, in a simple white garment, fragile, vulnerable, unadorned, a human being like any other. As the ceremony proceeded, this young woman gradually acquired the symbols of her fate, the sword of state, the orb and sceptre, the clothing, the robes, the jewels, and finally the crown, at which moment she was designated, by loud acclamation in the abbey, the custodian of God's purpose for a lifetime of duty and service. She was still a human being, but no longer one who could select her own responsibilities.

So, too, the custodians of Mewar are bound by an ethical imperative which is not of their choice; unlike with the monarchy in Britain, it is not one that is renewed by ceremony with each generation; it was pronounced by the guru Maharishi Harit Rashi in 734 when he pointed out the spiritual responsibility of service to others in entrusting Mewar to Bappa Rawal, and it has been inherited without question by every subsequent head of the family. Moreover, it is a duty that brings warmth and joyful satisfaction to the person who embraces it. Any psychiatrist will testify to the beneficent effects of true altruism, but spiritual guides were centuries ahead of psychiatrists in their understanding of this essential truth. (Psychiatrists are perhaps the modern descendants of gurus.) Marthanda Verma, the former Maharaja of Travancore, expressed the feeling of duty freely embraced in almost ecstatic terms. He spends ten minutes a day at the shrine of his deity Padmanabha—a time of solitary communion between ruler and custodian. What does he feel? "Gooseflesh", he said. "Everything is surrendered. It is a great, elating feeling. My hair stands on end with joy. Each and every time."

*   *   *   *

As we have seen in earlier chapters, this long tradition of service was threatened with, at best, irrelevance, or at worst, extinction, by the abolition in 1971 of all princely titles in contravention of a previously binding promise. Along with abolition came the withdrawal of all privileges, including legal immunity, the protection by state security, and of course Privy Purse funding. It was fortunate, to say the very least, that this devastating blow occurred during the lifetime of the last formally recognised ruler, Maharana Bhagwat Singh, for he was a man of extraordinary foresight and wisdom. The previous chapter relates how he anticipated events both by his creation of the institution of Maharana into a trust bearing that name in 1969, and by the terms of his last Will and Testament. The reader will recall the plaintive and intelligent emotion of his letter to Prime Minister Indira Gandhi reproduced on pp. 133–134, a document both of historical weight and moving depth: "Were it not for this love and confidence in us and our tradition of service, we would have ceased to exist long ago." Of the institution of Maharana, "I am merely its trustee and servant, for such a time as it pleases God…It is not my private possession. It belongs to the people." But such breathtaking eloquence would have little effect, as he must have known. So he turned his mind to the practical task of how to continue his responsibility of service in the absence of state revenues. As his son Arvind Singh Mewar has written, no constitution "can debar man from performing his duties to serve society." The question was, how? Arvind also wrote of his father, "In my recollection he never sought his own advantage in anything."

One possibility was automatically negated by the very nature of the Maharanas' tradition and historic vows to Ekling ji, as well as their direct accessibility to the people, and that was to enter the dubious world of political career and its inevitable juggling for influence. That would have been utterly hostile to the gentle administration of the Maharanas in the past without fear or favour. Arvind wrote, "It is assumed and expected that the Maharana is above party politics." Or, as the Maharaja of Travancore put it with his typical bluntness, "politics is a fickle mistress."

Maharana Bhagwat was thus faced with the need to make decisions which would bear long-term consequences, and it is here, of course, that the occasional comparisons we have made with the constitutional monarchy of Britain entirely collapse. Queen Elizabeth II is spared the necessity of decisions; they are all made for her, and her custodianship may be considered in this sense, symbolic. Bhagwat Singh and Arvind Singh had perforce to make their custodianship work in the modern world, and that meant bold initiatives—many of them.

The first and most obvious route was to develop Udaipur as a tourist attraction, in order to generate the funds that would be required for years to come if the inherited obligations of the family were to be properly embraced. The first step was Maharana Bhagwat's conversion of Jagniwas into the Lake Palace Hotel in 1963, a luxury destination now famous the world over and, since 1971, operated by the Taj Group. Following that, other palaces underwent similar adaptations and became jointly known as HRH Group of Hotels, under the direct control of the family and its administrative arm. It is now India's largest chain of heritage palaces, including no less than nine hotels, and it is the only one under private ownership. The hotels generate their own revenue, and are therefore self-supporting, but much more important than this is the fact that all profits in excess of operational requirements are used to fund the Maharana of Mewar Charitable Foundation, which in effect does the work that previous Maharanas did in person. Its growth over the twenty years which have elapsed since the first edition of this book was published has been phenomenal, and the scope of its endeavours too wide to summarize in a few pages. But a flavour of the many projects it has undertaken with astonishing verve and ambition must be attempted in order to show how Bappa Rawal's legacy is still kept marching forward some fourteen centuries later.

Using interest on the original substantial endowment from Bhagwat's purse, plus fees derived from entrance to the City Palace Museum, the Foundation was able immediately to invest in a programme of education for Udaipur's children, which must always be the source and fountain of all human potential. The Maharana Mewar Public School opened within the City Palace Complex in 1974, with 212 students. So successful was it that it expanded rapidly until it became necessary for Arvind to build another school outside the walls (Maharana Mewar Vidya Mandir), and today the two schools cater for more than 2,500 boys and girls. All are subsidized by the Foundation, and many are on complete scholarships without which their entire education would certainly have been impossible. There is even capacity for some to be boarded at the school in twin-bedded accommodations. Their school uniform, worn with evident pride when you spot them in the street, is a red and blue checkered shirt with the badge MMPS stitched on to the shirt pocket, a mandatory tie bearing the school logo, and beige trousers or skirts. Education for the welfare of the local population is now the passion of the heir to the House of Mewar, Lakshyaraj Singh Mewar, who makes it his personal promise to the future. In addition, the Foundation likewise provides for vocational training in carpentry, tailoring, metalwork, leatherwork and secretarial skills. It also maintains libraries and a research institute.

Then there is the matter of public health, as vital as education and historically one of the responsibilities of successive Maharanas. The charitable foundation provides for gyms and physical culture centres designed to promote awareness of health and hygiene, maintains orphanages and houses for people blighted by poverty, distributes food and clothing to those who might have neither, and helps to protect poor widows. All these philanthropic enterprises (which, it is worth pointing out, do not attract support from the State of India, nor is support ever sought), are not undertaken for any whimsical delight in 'doing good', but because they *have* to be done in accordance with the original vows made to the family deity under the instruction of their guru. No head of the House of Mewar would ever think himself entitled to respect if he were to neglect these responsibilities, nor would he attract the affection of the populace, which endures beyond and above any political rumbles which might trouble the country as a whole.

Perhaps no greater evidence of this continuing bond between *raja* and *praja* exists than the charitable dispensary which lies at the entrance to the City Palace Complex by the outer gate, Badi Pol. Manned by a team of medical professionals, it operates all year round and deals with more than 11,000 patients each year. Free medical treatment and medicines are given to those in need who would have no means of paying for advice, and social workers who distribute medicines in the countryside are reimbursed. The aged are offered unquestioning assistance and succour. The reason this medical aid is such an emotionally moving illustration of continuity is that the demands made upon the service are necessarily large, and each application for help must be considered by the dispensary in much the same way as, in eras past, it would have been considered by the Maharana. At root, nothing has really changed.

In Travancore, the situation which applies is different in degree, but identical in kind. The erstwhile ruling family has always spent on education, health, and housing for the poor. When asked to explain, the former maharaja replies with bold economy of words, "We do it because we want to do it." Selfish retention of resources for personal profit does not seem to cross his mind, an attitude entirely in keeping with his indifference to the call to convert his temple's treasure into money. Similarly, the commitment of the House of Mewar to their historical ethical code is total and unequivocal, and might well cause us to ponder in the current age of relentless greed and shallow ambition, in which fame, success and personal enrichment conspire to stifle all feeling for the common welfare. Moral values have been reduced, says the former ruler of Travancore, to "all about what do I get, not what do I do."

If medical services provided in Udaipur may serve as a touching display of communal care, then the attention given by the family to the problems of water management, not only for Udaipur, but for the entire region, is nothing short of spectacular.

It is virtually certain that none of the casual visitors who enjoy the soothing beauty of the Aravalli hills, of the lake and its palaces, or the frantic, smiling activity which throbs through the city of Udaipur, is aware that both the lake and the city are man-made. One should say 'lakes', because although Lake Pichola is the most visible and is assumed by everyone to be natural, it is one of eight interconnected lakes in the area, all of them created by successive Maharanas. The process was initiated by Rana Lakha when he constructed Lake Pichola across the river Sisarma between 1382 and 1385, in response to the need to guarantee water supply for his people, a crucial matter given the erratic nature of the local climate and the constant danger of drought. Two hundred years later, as the reader will remember from Chapter 4, having abandoned Chittor as ultimately indefensible, Rana Udai Singh decided to build a new capital in the protected basin of these hills. An old ascetic whom he encountered in the forest advised him to start a settlement at the end of the lake, and furthermore to enlarge the lake. At the time, nobody lived there; the city we know today did not evolve from an ancient settlement, but was founded, built and developed by the Maharana whose name it bears and who was the father of India's hero Rana Pratap. The founding is marked by a white stone inscribed in Hindi in the centre of the wide road leading up from the entrance gate to the Tripoliya Arch. The date is 1559.

Three years later, in 1562, Udai Singh built a dam across the river Ahar, known as the Udai Sagar, which represents the first-ever attempt in the world to improve the living standard of an entire population through management of a watershed area. Thus Udai Singh was the pioneer of watershed area planning, which, however seemingly dull and technical, was a revolutionary philanthropic act. It set the standard for future developments, as later Maharanas created further, smaller lakes and dams to effectively control the region's water supply with dramatic success, including the diversion of a river to feed the lake known as Jana Sagar by Rana Raj Singh. That was another first in the world, making Raj Singh the father of river diversion. But the culmination of all this imaginative engineering was the creation of the second largest lake, Fateh Sagar, a few miles to the north, by Maharana Fateh Singh, that impressive, saintly, noble and reflective man with whom this book began. He did more. A dam was constructed across the river Ahar to divert rainwater into Fateh Sagar Lake, which involved the construction of artificial canals and waterways of various designs to link up all the rivers and lakes in the basin.

The whole sequence of projects, spanning six centuries, is a triumph of engineering so cleverly worked out that, despite the lakes being at different points above sea-level and their waters having varying depths, their levels become uniform when they are all completely filled up, so that surplus water from one lake is automatically transferred to another by linkage. Professionals are constantly amazed. It is strange to realize that Maharana Fateh Singh, that man of quiet authority and spiritual grace whom even British pomposity could not disturb, should preside over the world's first-ever successful attempt at river linkage. Of course, he was no engineer himself, but the fact that he was responsible for such an ambitious project should cause no surprise; he was moved, as ever, by the need to maximize beneficial effects for his people, in accordance with his vows. To him, such an effort was natural and not to be wondered at.

Alas, the remorseless speed and scope of human advance over the last hundred years have brought problems that place this magnificent system in jeopardy. It is not difficult to identify the causes, which are manifold. The population has expanded, as in other parts of the world, towards a peak of sustainability; willful deforestation of the hills erodes the soil and silts up rivers and lakes; urban areas stretch to breaking point; the waters become polluted with excessive sewage and domestic waste, threatening cleanliness and hygiene; floating weeds, industrial pollutants and water-borne diseases cause constant anxiety. It is indeed ironic that all these problems are just as man-made as are the original marvel that they are despoiling.

With this in mind, the Maharana of Mewar Charitable Foundation has devoted enormous resources over the past few years to tackling these urgent problems with encouraging, even astonishing results. The control of environmental threats is one cause that greatly exercises Arvind Singh. "The sewage issue is very close to my heart", he has said. " I am trying my level best to devise ways of cleaning up the lakes, treating the sewage and pumping water into the lakes." Much progress has already been made, some of it quantifiable and indeed visible. For example, the construction of six 'green bridges' at Sukha Naka composed of natural bacteria, water-purifying plants and shrubs, stones and sand and coconut fibre, has rejuvenated Udai Sagar Lake and restored the ecology of the river Ahar, and thereby eliminated the foul smell that had so contaminated parts of the river and lakeside that it was impossible to stand in the vicinity for long. The water in the wells had been so bad that it was completely undrinkable, so much so that that even animals turned away from it. Vast quantities of foam accumulated under bridges and on shore. Now, the quality of ground water has improved so dramatically that it is wholly safe for drinking and cleansing purposes. The foam has disappeared. The smell has evaporated. Oxygen content in the water has rocketed. Algae developed in millions and, after many years, fish re-appeared in their thousands, feeding on the algae and plankton. Tortoises, water-snakes, worms have all returned and, with them, predator birds as well. Human beings can once more fish here with confidence. In short, the charity has achieved an almost miraculous reversal of what had been an ecological disaster through assiduous application of modern scientific methods and wisdom, and can point with pride to an environmental triumph. Thus does the welfare of the people continue to be upheld as a precious duty, and benevolence respected as the essence of life.

In return, the people of Udaipur rejoice every time the rains fall and the lake fills up. There is a spirit of elation in the city, a spring in every stride, a smile on every face. They all know that rainfall is their lifeblood, and its capture and control essential to their survival.

Another ecological experiment pioneered in India by the Foundation is the harnessing of solar energy for public transport. There are rickshaws in Udaipur which are now completely silent and clean, emitting no pollutants whatever, powered as they are by sun-trapping elements on their roofs. The Foundation has developed 14 prototypes of solar vehicles, as well as a boat, with the ultimate aim of making both the city and lake entirely free from transport dependent upon fossil fuels. This scheme led to the Foundation winning the European Solar Prize in Berlin (received by Lakshyaraj Singh Mewar).

It would be egregious to list here all the activities of the Maharana of Mewar Charitable Foundation, and perhaps prove too much for the general reader. The official closely-written and detailed catalogue runs to well over a hundred pages and includes the revival of ancient ritual celebrations which had fallen into disuse, to enhance the annual Holi Festival marking the arrival of Spring, and the launch of a long-term programme for conservation of the City Palace Museum with additional support and funding from the J. Paul Getty Foundation in Los Angeles, USA. Some of the projects so far completed are mentioned in the following chapter, which is devoted to this museum. The maintenance of some thirty temples in and around the city is another of the tasks undertaken.

I have left until now mention of one of the earliest activities of the Foundation, which was to institute an annual bestowal of awards to individuals who have given service of permanent value to society. This ceremony was started in 1980–81 and was initially limited in scope and number to students and school children for their academic achievements. Today there are 16 annual awards for different kinds of service, and over 3,700 recipients have received them in the intervening 30 years. Moreover, the awards have widened their geographical reach to national and even international levels. The international award is especially relevant as it honours a foreign national for his or her work in understanding the spirit and values of Mewar, and fiittingly, it is named after the first European to have chronicled the fabled history of this people—the Colonel James Tod Award. Winners have included the BBC correspondent Sir Mark Tully, the writer V.S. Naipaul, the novelist Mary Margaret Kaye (*The Far Pavilions*), and the actor and director Lord Attenborough.

In addition to these awards, in 2007 Arvind Singh established the Eternal Mewar website, dedicated to bringing the values of his unique ancestry to a worldwide audience, both to emphasize their continued relevance in the modern world, and to invite global participation in their promotion as, indeed, "eternal" values; people are encouraged not only to recognize the concept of custodianship, but to share in its future. He has thus, with vigour, furthered his father's ambition of bringing the ancient world surging into the present, and with new communication technology, far into the future. Bappa Rawal could not possibly have imagined any of this, but he would certainly have applauded it.

Two quite different events in recent years have demonstrated the potent emotional impact which Mewar's past continues to hold over the entire country. The first was the unveiling in 2009 of a mighty statue of the legendary Rana Pratap; the second was the truly majestic wedding of his descendant Padmaja, Arvind Singh's second daughter, in 2011.

The Dabok Airport outside Udaipur had already been re-named the Maharana Pratap Airport in 2004. Following this, the Foundation, in tandem with the HRH Group of Hotels and the national government, commissioned a statue to be placed outside the terminal building at the airport. It has to be said that this was very much the personal project of Arvind Singh whose involvement in all things to do with Mewar is known to be indefatigable. (Perhaps for this reason, he is known everywhere, with an indefinable mixture of affection and respect, as "Shriji", and his dignified bearing is appreciated by the people.) It was he who supervised every detail of the commission. He chose the sculptor, Fakir Chand Parida, and worked with him throughout the year it took to make, discussing the composition, advising on the battle attire to be worn by Pratap and on the size and shape of the horse Chetak's ears. It is now the largest, and many say the most imposing and poetic statue of Pratap in the whole country. For those interested in statistics, it is 14 feet long and 15 feet high, composed of gun-metal (copper, zinc, tin and lead), and weighs three thousand kilograms. Fittingly for a hero who now belongs beyond the boundaries of Mewar, this statue was unveiled by the President of India, Her Excellency Pratibha Devisingh Patil. This airport, by the way, can now boast more incoming flights than any other city in Rajasthan.

The wedding of Padmaja Kumari Mewar to Dr Kush Singh ji Parmar was celebrated with the fullest possible ritual according to ancient Vedic culture, with important (and, to a Westerner) mysterious daily ceremonies for a month before the final spectacle, which was a year in the preparation. Legions of people helped set the stage, and the resulting festivities, enjoyed by thousands, and including no less than eight sumptuous meals especially served in different courtyards and lawns of the palace grounds under special tents, each one a resplendent display of colour and culinary perfection, were beyond description. The final dinner, served at Shikarbadi, was attended by nearly four thousand people from the city, and the married couple received a parade of guests on a glittering stage for nearly three hours without pause. It was not only an event of great historic accuracy, but also the fond farewell of a father to his much-beloved daughter, and somehow the mixture of the personal with the spectacular made it all the more touching, as the present honoured the past, summed up in Arvind's gentle wave of the hand in blessing as the car carried the couple away down towards the palace gate and into their future; as they emerged, an impromptu band of townspeople gave a joyful display of song and dance.

If the wedding showed to some degree the ownership of Mewar's past by its people, a more eloquent testimony to this might well pass unnoticed, but it is nevertheless profound. As the restoration of the City Palace has proceeded, so has its 'recapture' by the people of Udaipur. New fountains have been put in place to ease the heat of the day, shaded areas for happy assembly have been built, benches and seating areas bid welcome to the visitor. Where once a few stray foreigners might have lingered and stared, the City Palace is now alive with throngs of people, an average of over two thousand every day. A minority of them are tourists from abroad, but astonishingly, 73% of them are Indian and many remain there all day long, simply enjoying possession of their shared national inheritance. For locals from Udaipur and the surrounding country it is much more than this. A man in town told the present writer that the head of the House of Mewar may live in the palace, but it is not his; it belongs to Ekling ji, and therefore to us. The belief is unwavering and apparently indestructible, and it is because this belief is as strong with a local tailor as it is with Arvind Singh Mewar himself, the feeling amongst the crowds within the City Palace, that this is actually *theirs*, is palpable and peculiarly resonant.

The bond will continue. Lakshyaraj Singh Mewar has not only the affection of the children at the school over the fortunes of which he presides, and the tenacious, even adoring, respect of the palace guards and military, who answer directly to him, but much more than that. Stories abound within the city of his kindness and care for people such as rickshaw drivers who might otherwise be ignored. Proof of this came when he undertook a pilgrimage to walk from the palace to the temple, a distance of some twenty-five miles. It took him five-and-a-half hours to complete the journey. Despite his intention not being officially announced, and word of it only drifting out a day in advance, thousands of people either joined him for part of the walk or lined the route for him, and everybody kept reaching out to hand him a drink of water on the way. Why? Because they knew he was going to Ekling ji, for them, and Ekling ji was as much their deity as his. The obeisance was shared. That was the whole point.

View of City Palace from Lake Pichola, Udaipur
The name Lake Pichola comes from the nearby small village of Picholi and was originally created early in the 15th century

Print designed by H. Clerget; Photograph by M.L. Rousselet
Acc. No. 2011.T.0024

THE CITY PALACE

Two difficulties attend any description of the City Palace in Udaipur. First, it is impossible to say who built it, as twenty-two Maharanas have built on and added to the palace they inherited, all the way from Udai Singh in the sixteenth century to Bhagwat Singh in the twentieth. When they ran out of space, they extended over the slope of the hill, supporting their structures on mighty props. Some have obviously contributed more than others, notably Amar Singh I (1597–1620), Karan Singh (1620–1628), Sangram Singh II (1710–1734), Sajjan Singh (1874–1884), and Fateh Singh (1884–1930). Even so, there is rarely a courtyard which does not bear the stamp of more than one monarch. Just take one example. The central area known as *Mor Chowk* was built by Karan Singh in the seventeenth century, but the inlaid glass mosaic work depicting peacocks, which are arguably its finest feature, were added by Sajjan Singh more than two hundred years later. As to the second difficulty, the very names are strange to Western ears and awkward to retain in the memory, so that it is too much to expect the first-time visitor to know whether the *Baadi Mahal* contains the *Amar Vilas*, or whether the *Chini-ki-chitra Sali* came before or after the *Krishna Vilas*. For both reasons, it is not only wise but essential to have a guide; if we attempted a description of each room here, it would be necessary to carry the book with one and attack its contents at every corner.

Not only that, but the interior design of the palace is so intricate and complex that it would be easy to get lost without a ball of string to record one's progress. From the outside, it is immediately apparent that the building had first to serve as a fortress. The lower levels are thick, stark, unyielding, windowless, one might even say featureless. Raise your eyes to the top, and you will see what Virginia Fass has vividly termed "a riot of canopies, kiosks, towers, ornamental turrets, and crenellations which give the effect of a fantastical icing on a massive cake." Once inside, however, one finds that the various peaks of this "icing" are connected by narrow passages and stairways which lead up, down, around, down, and up again, so that one entirely loses one's bearings.

There was one practical reason for this purposeful bewilderment. Any invader would not only find himself stranded with no idea how to escape, but would have room neither to wield a sword nor advance except in single file. But there is also a more whimsical explanation inherent in the very nature of the architecture. It lies in the desire to create a feeling of elusiveness. G.H.R. Tillotson captures it best:

> Its informal planning and massing creates a special quality... it does not concern the use of the buildings, it is a stylistic and sculptural quality and concerns the effect of a building on us, as observers, as we travel through it. The effect is to elude our immediate comprehension, to confuse or disorient us by means of complexity and ambiguity. The extensive and elaborate plan is so complicated that it cannot be considered all at once. Led from one portion of the palace to another by means of narrow, winding, enclosed corridors, we cannot easily establish how the various parts cohere. Even individual rooms contribute to this effect, they are rarely simply rectangular but tend to be of more complicated and unexpected shapes and we cannot see the whole of a particular room at once. Forests of columns reinforce this effect by obscuring our view of parts of rooms. And so the forms of individual rooms and the way in which they relate to each other are not clear or logical or easily readable.

In this context, Percy Brown has made a highly relevant reflection. "There is something more than architecture in these palaces", he writes. "Every stone is touched with the spirit of romance". In other words, the very mystery is not accidental, but intended. The supreme art of the Rajput architect is that he contrived to combine building with poetry.

Not so long ago, the scene in the great area outside the palace, after passing through the Tripoliya Gate, was one teeming with vitality. "At most hours of the day", says a guidebook published in 1909, "sacred bulls wander about at their ease, horses are being schooled, elephants move restlessly at their shackles, geese keep up a ceaseless conversation, and a myriad pigeons seem as much at home as in the Square of St Marks." Now, save for a few lingering geese, only the ghosts remain.

The question of the extent of Moghul influence is a vexed one. The cusped arch, long thought to be a Moghul invention, is now reckoned to have been used by Rajput craftsmen before the Moghuls arrived. Yet some conclusions are possible, relying solely on the eye. The Rajput palaces at Chittor and Kumbhalgarh are clearly masculine in feeling—tough, resilient, virile, and relatively unadorned. Moghul influence brought a delicacy of touch and refinement of decoration which are much lighter and are characterised by the beautiful inlaid glass-work and mosaics which add prettiness to the gloriously gentle proportions of the Lake Palace. The Moghuls had a passion for smothering interior surfaces "in a calculated chaos of geometric patterns." But the Lake Palace was intended as a domestic residence for the summer months, not as a military stronghold. At the City Palace one may see both—the hard, practical solidity of the initial fortress, graced by the subtle richness of later additions made in times of peace.

All these palaces are to be experienced rather than merely gazed upon. They are eloquent witnesses to the life held within them—a life of grandeur and nobility, of ritual and formality, of tradition and honour. It is a life that will not return.

Not all the City Palace is a museum of the past. Great areas are used by the Maharana of Mewar Charitable Foundation, as mentioned in the foregoing text. There is also the school and Technical Institute, a free Dispensary and a Library, and the Maharana Mewar Research Institute. Other portions are occupied by the Government of Rajasthan, including a Museum of Archaeology. This latter houses very important archives of the Mewar dynasty, of which over one thousand documents are inscribed on copper and date back as far as the reign of Maharana Kumbha. All of this is now available to selected scholars.

The motor-car enthusiast would do well to take a look also at the Palace Garage attached to Garden Hotel in Udaipur City. Here he will find an array of old vehicles many of which have their own historical significance. The 1940 open-top Cadillac was presented to Maharana Bhupal Singh by the Maharaja of Bikaner on the occasion of Bhagwat Singh's marriage. Bhupal Singh liked to use it so that the people could see him on his rare sorties outside the palace walls. It is still used on very special occasions, as for the visit of Queen Elizabeth II. There is also a convertible Rolls-Royce dating from 1924 which Bhupal used in his last years. Of the seven Rolls-Royces he maintained, three are left, and one was used in the James Bond film *Octopussy*. In addition, there are another two Cadillacs, one Buick, a Rambler, various smaller cars, and three Mercedes. One of these, a 1956 model, holds a unique place in the affections of the family. Maharana Bhagwat Singh used it once a week only, for his regular Monday evening visit to Ekling ji. It has never been used for any other purpose, and is referred to as "Ekling ji's car".

Since the first edition of this book, manifold additions have been made to the exhibits on view in the City Palace Museum, and renovations to the intricate mosaics, glasswork and tile work have brought sparkle and life to a building which might otherwise have echoed only with the soft breath of ghosts. The most dramatic renovation has been the completion of the majestic Tripoliya, the triple-arched entrance to the palace site from the town. Built in white marble by Maharana Sangram Singh II in 1711, it was intended that massive wooden doors should complete the arches, through the central one of which only the Maharana himself passed. But they were never constructed. Three centuries later, the 76th Custodian Arvind Singh Mewar commissioned the doors finally to be made with Burma teak wood and brass fittings, using entirely the skills of local craftsmen. The central door alone weighs 4400 kilograms.

Domestic furnishings have been brought out of storage to reveal how rooms were once used, including the space where Maharanas gave audience and received requests from the people, and especially the private rooms of Arvind Singh's grandmother, wife to the invalid Maharana Bhupal Singh. Bhupal, described by one of the townspeople as "a small man with a very big heart", would be delighted to know that local people now come in their thousands to sit and talk and rest within the walls of what had been his home.

Perhaps the most impressive exhibit is a small portion of the collection of photographs dating onwards from 1860, rescued from dozens of boxes and painstakingly catalogued. 27,000 photographs and over 1,000 glass negatives make this one of the most important such collections in India. Walking through these galleries one feels that the past and the present fuse, and that the Maharanas are still watching, thoughtfully.

Dosti London coins

GENEALOGICAL LIST OF THE RULERS OF MEWAR

(Dates refer to the period of reign)

1.	Guhil (Guhaditya)	566–586
2.	Bhoj	586–606
3.	Mahendra	606–626
4.	Naag (Nagaditya)	626–646
5.	Shiladitya	646–661
6.	Aparajit	661–688
7.	Mahendra II	688–734
8.	BAPPA RAWAL (Kalbhoj)	734–753
9.	Khuman I	753–773
10.	Mattut	773–793
11.	Bharatribhatt I	793–813
12.	Sinha	813–828
13.	Khuman II	828–853
14.	Mahayak	853–878
15.	Khuman III	878–942
16.	Bharatribhatt II	942–943
17.	Allat	951–953
18.	Narvahan	971–973
19.	Salivahan	973–977
20.	Shaktikumar	977–993
21.	Ambaprasad	993–1007
22.	Shuchiverma	1007–1021
23.	Narverma	1021–1035

24.	Kirtiverma	1035–1051
25.	Yograj	1051–1068
26.	Vairath	1068–1088
27.	Hanspal	1088–1103
28.	Vair Singh	1103–1107
29.	Vijai Singh	1107–1127
30.	Ari Singh I	1127–1138
31.	Chaudh Singh	1138–1148
32.	Vikram Singh	1148–1158
33.	Run Singh	1158–1168
34.	Kshem Singh	1168–1172
35.	Samant Singh	1172–1179
36.	Kumar Singh	1179–1191
37.	Mathan Singh	1191–1211
38.	Padam Singh	1211–1213
39.	Jaitra Singh	1213–1253
40.	Tej Singh	1261–1267
41.	Samar Singh	1273–1302
42.	Ratan Singh (Last of the Rawal Family)	1303
43.	Maharana Hamir Singh I	1326–1364
44.	Maharana Kshetra Singh	1364–1382
45.	Maharana Lakha	1382–1421
46.	Maharana Mokal	1421–1433
47.	Maharana Kumbha	1433–1468
48.	Maharana Ooda Singh	1468–1473
49.	Maharana Raimal	1473–1509
50.	Maharana Sangram Singh I (Sanga)	1509–1527
51.	Maharana Ratan Singh II	1527–1531

52.	Maharana Vikramaditya	1531–1536
53.	Maharana Udai Singh II	1537–1572
54.	Maharana Pratap Singh I	1572–1597
55.	Maharana Amar Singh I	1597–1620
56.	Maharana Karan Singh	1620–1628
57.	Maharana Jagat Singh I	1628–1652
58.	Maharana Raj Singh I	1653–1680
59.	Maharana Jai Singh	1680–1698
60.	Maharana Amar Singh II	1698–1710
61.	Maharana Sangram Singh II	1710–1734
62.	Maharana Jagat Singh II	1734–1751
63.	Maharana Pratap Singh II	1751–1753
64.	Maharana Raj Singh II	1754–1761
65.	Maharana Ari Singh II	1761–1773
66.	Maharana Hamir Singh II	1773–1778
67.	Maharana Bhim Singh	1778–1828
68.	Maharana Jawan Singh	1828–1838
69.	Maharana Sardar Singh	1838–1842
70.	Maharana Swarup Singh	1842–1861
71.	Maharana Shambhu Singh	1861–1874
72.	Maharana Sajjan Singh	1874–1884
73.	Maharana Fateh Singh	1884–1930
74.	Maharana Bhupal Singh	1930–1955
75.	Maharana Bhagwat Singh	1955–1984
76.	Shriji Arvind Singh Mewar	1984

LIST OF BRITISH POLITICAL AGENTS AND RESIDENTS IN MEWAR

Col. James Tod	1818–1822
Captain Cobbe	1822–1830
Major Spear	1830–1834
Major Robinson	1839–1845
Lt-Col. Lawrence	1850–1857
Captain Showers	1857–1860
Major Taylor	1860–1862
Lt-Col. Eden	1862–1865
Major Nixon	1865–1867
Lt-Col. Hutchinson	1868–1869
Lt-Col. Nixon	1869–1872
Lt-Col. Hutchinson	1872–1874
Major Bradford	1874
Lt-Col. Wright	1874–1875
Col. Herbert	1875–1876
Lt-Col. Impey	1876–1878
Major Cadell	1878–1879
Lt-Col. Walter	1879–1881

POLITICAL AGENTS BECAME
RESIDENTS AFTER 1881

Dr Stratton	1881–1882
Lt-Col. Euan Smith	1882
Lt-Col. Walter	1882–1885
Lt-Col. Biddulph	1885
Mr Plowden	1885–1886
Mr Wingate	1886
Lt-Col. Euan Smith	1886
Lt-Col. Walter	1886–1887
Col. Miles	1887–1889
Lt-Col. Peacock	1889
Major Fraser	1889–1890
Lt-Col. Peacock	1890
Lt-Col. Abbott	1890
Col. Miles	1890–1893
Lt-Col. Martelli	1893
Lt-Col. Wyllie	1893–1894
Col. Prideaux	1894
Lt-Col. Wyllie	1894–1896
Lt-Col. Newiil	1896–1897
Lt-Col. Revenshaw	1897–1899
Lt-Col. Yate	1899–1900
Lt-Col. Thornton	1900

Captain Pinhey	1900–1902
Mr Blakesley	1902
Major Pinhey	1902–1906
Captain Drumond	1906
Mr Claude Hill	1906–1907
Captain Chevenix Trench	1907
Mr Claude Hill	1907–1908
Captain Chevenix Trench	1908
Mr Holme	1908–1911
Lt-Col. Kaye	1911–1913
Mr Holland	1913
Lt-Col. Kaye	1913–1914
Mr Glancy	1914
Lt-Col. Kaye	1914–1915
Major Drummond	1915
Lt-Col. Kaye	1915–1916
Mr Russell	1916
Mr Home	1916–1919
Lt-Col. Spence	1919–1920
Lt-Col. Macpherson	1920
Mr Wilkinson	1920–1922
Mr Wilkinson	1922–1924
Major Pritchard	1924–1925
Major Ogylvie	1925–1927
Major Bisco	1927

Mr Mackenzie	1927–1928
Lt-Col. Grabier	1928
Mr Lothian	1930–1931
Lt-Col. Macnabb	1931–1933
Lt-Col. Garstin	1933–1935
Lt-Col. Batham	1935–1938
Lt-Col. Barton	1938–1939
Mr Todd	1940–1941
Mr Trevelyan	1941–1942
Lt-Col. Williams	1942–1943
Lt-Col. Kirkbridge	1943–1947

SOURCES AND BIBLIOGRAPHY

1. MANUSCRIPT

Archives of the Maharana Mewar Research Institute, City Palace, Udaipur.

Memoirs (unpublished) of the late Maharana Bhagwat Singh.

Letters from the Royal Archives, Windsor Castle, England.

Letters from Sir Charles Euan-Smith, British Library, India Office, London.

2. MEWAR

The indispensable source for anyone interested in researching the Mewar dynasty must be James Tod's *Annals and Antiquities of Rajasthan*, to which I have had frequent recourse in the present narrative. Not only a painstaking work of reference—the first to bring this history to light in the West, it is also a masterpiece of literature in its own right. Other books of associated interest include:

B.D. Agarwal, *Udaipur* (Rajasthan District Gazetteers, 1979)

J.S. Armour, *The Glories of Mewar* (1936)

Battle of Haldighati (Maharana Pratap Smarak Samiti, Udaipur, 1976)

J.C. Brookes, *History of Mewar* (1859)

Sir Conrad Corfield, *Memories of Princely India*

Hugh Davenport, *Udaipur: The Trials and Triumphs of the Mewar Kingdom*

A.N. Day, *Mewar under Maharana Kumbha 1433–1468* (1978)

K.S. Gupta, *Mewar and Maratha Relations* (1971)

D.R. Mankekar, *Sisodia's Role in Indian History* (1976)

Maharana Bhupal Singh Mewar (Pratap Shodh Pratisthan, 1984)

B.S. and J.S. Mehta, *Pratap the Patriot*

B.S. and J.S. Mehta, *Chittorgarh: The Cradle of Chivalry and Culture* (Rajasthan Itihas Parishad, Udaipur)

Fateh Lal Mehta, *Handbook of Mewar*

J.S. Mehta, *Abu to Udaipur*

T.K. Mathur, *Feudal Polity in Mewar* (Jaipur, 1987)

D.L. Paliwal, *Mewar and the British* (1971)

Report on the Administration of Mewar State for the years 1940, 1941 and 1942 (Madras Law Journal Press, 1944)

G.N. Sharma, *Glories of Mewar*

G.N. Sharma, *Lecture of Mughal Influence in Mewar* (1953)

G.N: Sharma, *Mewar and the Mughal Emperors* (1954)

Short Notes on Interesting Places in Udaipur (1909)

Kesri Singh, *Haldighati: Symbol of the Spirit of Independence* (1976)

Udaipur 1885–1921 (The Times Press, 1921)

Udaipur and its Ruler (Times of India Press, 1929)

Udaipur (The Preservation of National Monuments, India Office, London)

D.C. Sircar, *The Guhilas of Kishkindha* (Sanskrit College, Calcutta, 1965)

Ram Vallabh Somani, *History of Mewar* (Jaipur, 1976)

G.E.C. Wakefield, *Recollections: 50 Years in the Service of India* (Civil and Military Gazzette, Lahore, 1942)

3. RAJASTHAN

Francis Brunei, *Rajasthan* (Roli Books, New Delhi)

Rosa Maria Cimino, *Life at Court in Rajasthan* (Florence, 1985)

Michael Edwardes, *Indian Temples and Palaces* (Hamlyn, London, 1969)

Virginia Fass, *The Forts of India*

Virginia Fass and the Maharajah of Baroda, *The Palaces of India*

Naveen Patnaik, *A Second Paradise: Indian Courtly Life 1590–1947* (Rupa, Calcutta; Sigwick & Jackson, London, 1985)

Dasharatha Sharma, *Rajasthan through the Ages* (Bikaner, 1966)

Andrew Topsfield, *Paintings From Rajasthan in the National Gallery of Victoria* (1980)

Andrew Topsfield, in *Oriental Art*, Vol. 30, No.4 (1984)

R. Singh, *Rajasthan: India's Enchanted Land*

4. GENERAL

J.R. Ackerley, *Hindoo Holiday* (Chatto & Windus, London, 1932)

Charles Allen, *Lives of the Indian Princes* (Century, London, 1984)

Charles Allen, *Plain Tales from the Raj*

Evelyn Battye, *Customs and Characters of the British Raj*

Percy Brown *Indian Architecture* (Bombay, 1972)

J. Fergusson, *History of India and Eastern Architecture* (London, 1899)

J. Fergusson, *Picturesque Illustrations of Ancient Architecture in Hindustan* (London, 1848)

Bamber Gascoigne, *The Great Moghuls* (1971)

Handbook of India (Central Publicity Bureau, Government of India Railway Department)

Ved Mehta, *Portrait of India*

V.P. Menon, *The Story of the Integration of the Indian States* (Orient Longmans, 1956)

Geoffrey Moorhouse, *India Britannica* (Harvill, London, 1983)

Ann Morrow, *Highness* (Grafton, London, 1986)

Tim Piggot-Smith, *Out of India* (Constable, London, 1986)

Amaury de Riencourt, *The Soul of India* (Cape, London, 1961)

G.H.R. Tillotson, *The Rajput Palaces*